'Every Special Education Program in the New York City public school system features classes with "Activities for Daily Living". Included, and of particular importance, are cookery classes. *The Cookbook for Children with Special Needs* is therefore an extremely valuable tool for such classes. A consistent tone of encouragement, along with the logical transition of learning about food and safety in the kitchen, and the step-by-step procedure for each recipe, makes this book a "must-have" for teachers. In addition, the photographs, illustrations and space for comments creates a kid-oriented focus. It is an excellent guide for educators, parents and teachers alike.'

– Margo Donovan, Staff Developer,
New York City Department of Special Education

'For children with special needs, being involved in the kitchen can help overcome difficulties in various areas including: fine motor issues, difficulties with concentration and sensory, cognitive and emotional issues such as low self-esteem… The emotional reward for a child experiencing a sense of responsibility by being entrusted with the task of preparing food allows the child to blossom with immeasurable satisfaction and pride. In this informative and enjoyable book, Deborah French has enabled families with children with special needs, to spend time together doing fun and simple everyday activities in an easy and graded way. I would highly recommend it for all children!'

– Benita Rochberger, Developmental and
Cognitive Occupational Therapist

'I've learnt so many things… Debbie's taught me how to make soups, chicken, burgers, chocolate cupcakes and loads more. I love taking a bite of what I've made and thinking, "Wow! This is heaven!"'

– Liora, aged twelve

'Liora has grown proficient and confident in many areas of food preparation and cookery.'

– Emma, mother of Liora

'Debbie has taught me to make really tasty and good food and different and new ways of preparing food. She has also taught me to be careful with the oven, gas, top, etc. I have learnt to be organised in the kitchen and to tidy up after myself. We even add our own ideas to the cooking, if it is suitable, which I love.'

– Tom, aged eleven

of related interest

Asanas for Autism and Special Needs
Yoga to Help Children with their Emotions,
Self-Regulation and Body Awareness
Shawnee Thornton
ISBN 978 1 84905 988 6
eISBN 978 1 78450 059 7

Simple Low-Cost Games and Activities
for Sensorimotor Learning
A Sourcebook of Ideas for Young Children
Including Those with Autism, ADHD, Sensory Processing
Disorder, and Other Learning Differences
Lisa A. Kurtz
ISBN 978 1 84905 977 0
eISBN 978 0 85700 879 4

Gardening for Children with Autism Spectrum
Disorders and Special Educational Needs
Engaging with Nature to Combat Anxiety, Promote
Sensory Integration and Build Social Skills
Natasha Etherington
ISBN 978 1 84905 278 8
eISBN 978 0 75700 599 1

Fun with Messy Play
Ideas and Activities for Children
with Special Needs
Tracey Beckerleg
ISBN 978 1 84310 641 8
eISBN 978 1 84642 854 8

The Cookbook for Children with Special Needs

Learning a Life Skill with Fun, Tasty, Healthy Recipes

DEBORAH FRENCH

ILLUSTRATED BY LEAH EHRLICH

Jessica Kingsley *Publishers*
London and Philadelphia

First published in 2015
by Jessica Kingsley Publishers
73 Collier Street
London N1 9BE, UK
and
400 Market Street, Suite 400
Philadelphia, PA 19106, USA

www.jkp.com

Copyright © Deborah French 2015
Illustration copyright © Leah Ehrlich 2015
Photography copyright © Zara Brooks 2015

Library of Congress Cataloging in Publication Data
A CIP catalog record for this book is available from the Library of Congress

British Library Cataloguing in Publication Data
A CIP catalogue record for this book is available from the British Library

ISBN 978 1 84905 538 3
eISBN 978 1 78450 156 3

Printed and bound in China

This book is dedicated to Henry, Amariah, Elisheva and Rafaella.

You are our inspiration and the lights of our lives.

With love.

'The medicine to take the ASD away is always teaching and listening.'

Henry French, aged ten

Contents

Acknowledgements   9

Introduction   11
For the Parents and Guardians of Children and
Young Adults with Special Needs

1. The Story of Food   15

2. Keeping Safe   48

3. Getting Started   59
Equipment   59
Icon and Skill Glossary   66
Recipe Layout and Explanation   81

THE RECIPES

Level One Recipes   85
Peckish Pita Pieces   86
Baker's Bread   89
Double Bedded Eggs   93
Cheesy Popeye Pancakes   96
Loaded Potatoes   99
Minestrone Madness   102
Farfallino Pasta   105
Fruit Mountain   109
Sticky Chocolate Cornflakes   112
Aunty Deb's Choc Chunk Cookies   115

Level Two Recipes   119

Pizza: The Italiano   120
Creamy Scrambled Eggs with Smoked Salmon   124
Quick Mushroom and Pea Risotto   127
Crispy Mac 'n' Cheese   130
Lentil Soup with Cheesy Garlic Bread   134
Ocean Fishcakes   138
Fish Fingers with Wild West Wedges   142
Classic Victoria Sponge   146
Vanilla Ice Cream   150
Gooey Chocolate Brownies   153

Level Three Recipes   157

Simply Perfect Roast Chicken with Basmati Rice   158
Classic Chicken Noodle Soup   161
Crunchy Chicken with Sweet and Sour Cabbage   165
Creamy Chicken Sandwich   169
The Ultimate Burger   172
Bolognese   175
Honey-Roasted Turkey with Sweet Potato Mash   179
Crunchy Apple and Raspberry Crumble   183
Cinnamon Pancakes with Maple Syrup Butter   186
My First Chocolate Cake   189

Menu Ideas   193

Index   196

Acknowledgements

The research for writing this cookery book began in the 1980s, during my early years. The kitchen in the house where I grew up was the hub of our family life and, being a food lover, this is where I enjoyed spending most of my time.

I can still recall buzzing with excitement after my mother said I could bake my favourite chocolate cake on a Sunday afternoon. It is an absolute joy for me to be able to present that same recipe as my final dessert in this book.

To Mum and Dad: You taught me to value the importance of family mealtimes. I learnt to appreciate and enjoy so many different types of food, even a nut loaf! And even now as you follow a vegan diet, I'm constantly inspired by you both. Mum, every meal that you serve is an art form: the table is always set beautifully, the food is presented perfectly. You taught me that we eat with our eyes and it is this principle that has shaped my food preparation and teaching ever since. I thank you for ingraining in me such an integral part of everyday life, and I am indebted to you both for your relentless support and guidance in everything that I do.

To my husband, Johnny: Nothing would be possible without you. I love you and thank you for your tireless support and advice throughout the writing of this book. My orange folder has been a staple part of our home from day one. You've endured tasting hundreds of my experiments and I have felt your love throughout, even through the disasters. I am grateful to you every second of every day.

To my chief tasters, Henry, Amariah, Elisheva and Rafaella: Life is so wonderful now that you are in it. This book would never have come to fruition without your thoughts and opinions on my food. You, too, worked so hard to help this book come to fruition; it is a celebration of our fun. I love sharing our kitchen together and I can't wait to see and taste all your experiments as you grow up. I love you all and am profoundly grateful to God for blessing our lives with you.

To my mother- and father-in-law: Mum, you have introduced me to a world of spices, chilli and flavours I never thought I could tolerate. You have taught me to explore and try new tastes while making sure everything I make is quick, efficient and absolutely delicious. Cooking together is a joy and it was you who encouraged me to teach, which set me on the path I love and for which I am deeply grateful. Johnny and I appreciate everything that both you and Dad do for us and our family.

To my brother, Ben: You hit the jackpot when you married your beautiful wife, Debbie, and I am indebted to you for giving me the sister I never had.

Debbie: There is not one meal in the past 13 years that we haven't discussed. I have no idea how this book would have come into being without your advice, recipe contributions and guidance. Thank you for patience, testing and opinions. Thank you for caring that much, and I can't wait to have many more years writing menu plans with you.

To my brother, Elliot, and darling Natasha: Thank you for all your love and support, always. Living so far away, we greatly miss spending time with you and your gorgeous children. I love exploring food tastes with you both and especially enjoy and appreciate your food photography on nights out!

To Leah, my incredible illustrator: You are so talented. Not only are your drawings fabulous, you are able to take a page of my notes, understand them and visualize them perfectly. It is a pleasure to work with you and I hope to have the opportunity to continue to do so in the future. Find out more information about Leah's work at www.monalisasart.com.

Thank you to Lisa Salaminov for getting me started on developing my confidence in food styling.

To Zara, my photographer: Your pictures are perfection and your great eye and style helped to make this book beautiful. Downpours and grey skies were no match for your talent and our determination. Thank you for all your hard work. For more information on Zara's work, please contact her at brooks2@bezeqint.net.

To my editor, Lucy Buckroyd, and the editorial and design teams at Jessica Kingsley Publishers: Thank you for believing in me and presenting me with a lifetime opportunity to fulfil my dream of writing and publishing my first cookery book.

Introduction

For the Parents and Guardians
of Children and Young Adults
with Special Needs

I spent countless hours in the waiting rooms of doctors and therapists during my children's early years. At the age of two my eldest son, Henry, was diagnosed with autistic spectrum disorder, six months after his sister, Amariah, was born with Down syndrome.

It became almost impossible to differentiate between the assessments and therapy sessions. The summaries for Henry were always the same: low muscle tone and hypermobility, coupled with poor gross motor skills, delayed development and echolalic speech. I purchased every type of special scissors, pencil grips and block sets on the market to help develop my son's poor fine motor skills. Nothing made a difference; we transitioned from the early years into primary school with the same problems.

One cold winter's day when Henry was four years old, we decided to bake cookies. I purchased supersized cookie cutters to help compensate for clumsy fingers. Yet, while at work in the kitchen, I was surprised that Henry's movements were controlled and attentive. His cookie shapes were immaculate.

I barely made any cookies that afternoon; I simply watched Henry with a quizzical brow as he worked. Every evaluation we had received in his four years had stated clearly that Henry was unable to concentrate for longer than five minutes on any given task. As a tray of freshly baked cookies came out of the oven, I realized that in the kitchen Henry's concentration and fine motor skills were excellent.

I was angst-ridden the day I allowed Henry to use a kitchen knife. After a month of continuously baking cookies, I took a giant leap of faith and watched as Henry followed my careful instructions and prepared a salad. There was not a chopped finger in sight! Henry sliced cucumbers, peppers and tomatoes; he was calm and attentive throughout. It was so exciting to see his elation after preparing the final dish. We ate salad for weeks after that day, whether we wanted to or not! It was clear that Henry loved being in the kitchen; it calmed him, channelled his energy and gave him a wonderful sense of achievement.

From that moment on, my children's participation in the kitchen never stopped. There was always either a chair or stepping stool next to me while I worked, and Henry's early play dates consisted of pancake frying or cookie cutting. More and more children wanted to be involved and their parents started to ask if their children could learn how to cook too.

I opened my first cookery class in my home for all children when Henry was nine years old, paving the way for the development of my cookery course for children and young adults with special needs.

Learning how to cook is an essential life skill that boosts self-confidence and develops individuality and creativity in all who try it. Those with special needs are no exception, and proficiency in the kitchen will play a key role in their independence as adults.

The Cookbook for Children with Special Needs has been written to help your children understand the origins of the food we eat, how the ingredients we use create our diet and how this affects our health and the way that we feel. The opening story introduces our primary theme, which is that we are all responsible for the choices we make about the foods that we eat.

The Cooking Process

We examine:

- how ingredients are combined to create a meal
- the benefits of cooking

- the health and safety pitfalls, coupled with step-by-step rules and regulations to keep you safe, including where and how produce needs to be stored

- how to use a recipe.

The Recipes

A colour-coded Icon and Skill Glossary leads on to 30 recipes, which are divided into three levels. There are ten recipes in each level, seven of which are savoury and three of which are sweet. The focus on savoury dishes reinforces the importance of moderation in our diet, ensuring that our primary foods are healthy ones and that our indulgent foods are exactly that.

The Icon and Skill Glossary visually demonstrates how specific skills are performed in the kitchen. Icons are printed alongside each step in the recipes, reminding the reader of the skills they need. The colour code allows easy access to the glossary if needed.

Each recipe is divided into steps to make it easier to follow the order of activity. Furthermore, children are prompted throughout to seek help from an adult if they feel unsure of what to do. It is recommended that each recipe is reviewed by an adult prior to the child attempting the recipe, for each child's capabilities and restrictions are individual. This way the parent will be able to determine where extra help maybe needed. This includes preparing equipment and ingredients. At the end of each recipe the child has room to write their thoughts or comments. For example, they may wish to use mushrooms instead of tomatoes in the dish next time. The reader is thus encouraged to explore their own creativity, their likes and dislikes.

The Cookbook for Children with Special Needs is skill orientated rather than being divided into starters, mains and desserts. The recipes introduce adult dishes to children and young adults, and while the photographs are sophisticated to make the reader feel more grown up, the recipes themselves are child friendly to enable them to become successful cooks.

The Levels

Level One contains basic recipes, using store cupboard staple ingredients for everyday sustenance, such as soup and bread. It introduces basic cooking skills: how to use a knife, frying and boiling, for example.

In Level Two similar ingredients are used but in a more sophisticated way. The skills introduced in Level One are practised in order to develop ability, and readers are shown how different dishes can be created from the same foodstuffs as those used in Level One. By repeating the use of the same ingredients in Level Two that were introduced in Level One, children learn how to reuse ingredients in different ways to create different dishes. This in turn helps children to learn to keep within a budget by using up the ingredients they have rather than simply shopping again.

Level Three introduces meat and chicken. Once again, all the skill sets are reintroduced as repetition is so important. The reader should follow the course from start to finish in order to maximize their ability.

Finally, dishes from across the three levels are used to create a suggested menu list.

Measurements and Heat

Measuring cups and spoons, rather than metric measurements, are standard throughout the book as these are the easiest methods of measurement for children with special needs.

Oven temperatures are for a Celsius oven or Fahrenheit equivalent unless stated otherwise. If using a Celsius fan oven, temperatures should be decreased by 20 degrees Celsius (36 degrees Fahrenheit).

Have fun cooking!

Deborah French

Chapter 1
The Story of Food

Where does food come from?

Food comes from

animals

and plants.

Cows live on a farm

and are looked after by a farmer.

Fish live in the sea

and are caught by fishermen.

Apples are a fruit
and they are
picked from trees.

Potatoes are a
vegetable and they
grow as a plant in
the ground.

Grains such as
wheat, corn and
rye are grown
in fields and are
harvested by
farmers.

Some people like to grow their own
fruits and vegetables in the garden

and cook them fresh in their kitchen.

Before certain foods can be eaten, they need to be changed in some way.

Milk comes from a cow,

then it is cleaned in a special factory

ready for us to drink.

Whole fish are cleaned,

then cut and cooked
in an oven

ready for us to eat.

Whole apples

are washed and juiced

to make apple juice.

Whole grains are gathered into bales,

ground into flour and cooked in the oven

to make fresh bread.

Different foods are known as ingredients. Ingredients can be eaten separately or mixed together in a variety of ways to make a meal or a diet.

Around the world, each country uses ingredients in different ways to create their traditional diet. Here are some examples:

UNITED KING

AMERICA

ARGENTINA

SOUTH

MIDDLE EAST

JAPAN

INDIA

CA

AUSTRALIA

Let's take a closer look...

Milk, flour, cream, fruit and tea are combined to create the traditional English tea.

Chicken, rice and spices are combined to create India's traditional curry.

Sugar, milk, egg, cream and fruit are mixed together to create Australia's traditional Pavlova dessert.

Chickpeas, flour, seasonings and oil are combined to create the traditional diet across the Middle East.

Chicken, flour and seasonings create the traditional American hot dog.

Fish, rice, vegetables and seaweed are combined to create Japan's traditional sushi meal.

How do we create our own diet
so that we are healthy and strong?

Bread, Rice,
Pasta, Potatoes

Milk & Dairy
Foods

Fruits & Vegetables

Meat, Fish,
Beans, Eggs

Drink
gar/fat

The Eat Well plate divides food into five
groups. Each group is a different size,
showing us how much we should eat from

Each food group gives our bodies a variety of nutrients and vitamins that help look after different parts of our bodies.

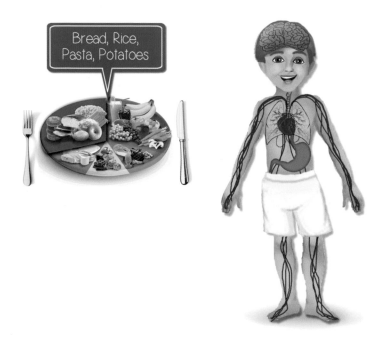

Wholegrain carbohydrates help our bodies feel fuller for longer, which gives our brains more energy to concentrate in school.

Fruits and vegetables help to prevent illness and are essential for a healthy heart and muscles.

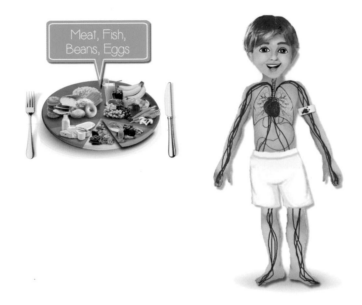

Proteins give our bodies minerals that keep our blood healthy and help to heal wounds too.

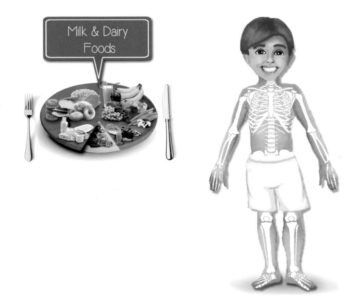

Dairy foods are rich in calcium, a mineral that is very important for healthy teeth and bones.

Sweets, chocolates, crisps and fizzy drinks taste good but they do very little to keep our bodies strong and healthy. That is why we should only eat a very small amount.

Now that we understand the role of each food group, let's see the effects of the choices we make when we eat.

Did you know that the strongest athletes in the world love to eat fruits and vegetables?

Athletes need to be fit and healthy. Their muscles work hard to help them succeed in their sport.

Athletes think very carefully about the foods they can eat to help them be as strong as possible.

Let's take a closer look...

David is an athlete and needs to make sure that each day he has a healthy and balanced diet to keep him strong enough to play basketball.

Look at how many fruits and vegetables he eats in a day!

He drinks water and herbal teas and eats lots of carbohydrates and proteins to help him concentrate and keep his muscles strong.

Breakfast   Lunch   Snack   Dinner

Julia is a gymnast and enjoys very similar foods to David.

Mealtimes are filled with fruits and vegetables, carbohydrates, proteins and dairy foods to keep Julia fit and able to concentrate when she is balancing on the beam.

What do you think would happen to David if he chose to change his diet and eat differently?

Here David has swapped water for fizzy drinks, fruits and vegetables for crisps and chocolates. They taste great, but...

...sugary foods don't have enough vitamins and minerals to keep David strong and healthy. His heart has to work harder because there is less energy in the food he eats.

David can't run or jump high enough to play basketball well.

What if Julia thought that succeeding on the beam meant that her body had to be very small?

How do you think Julia would feel if she ate no food for breakfast and very little for lunch and dinner?

Eating very little food has taken all of Julia's energy and strength away. Her uniform is now too big because her body is smaller and she is not fit enough to practise her routine.

Eating well is a choice that every person needs to make in order to have the best chance at a long and healthy life.

Learning how to cook helps us to make good food choices.

Cooking is the word that is used to describe the process of preparing, mixing and heating different ingredients together to make a meal.

Let's take a closer look...

To cook, we take different
fresh ingredients,

wash some of them with
water to make them clean,

change the way they look, and

mix them together with heat

to create a meal that we can eat and enjoy.

A cook is someone who learns how to make meals using different tools and skills.

Everybody can learn how to cook, all that is needed is a little patience and attention.

A mother or father in their kitchen at home prepares meals for their family.

A chef works in a restaurant and prepares many different types of meals for his customers.

All children and young adults can learn the skills to create delicious food in the kitchen.

There are many benefits to learning how to cook.

Cooking helps you to make good food choices because you can decide and prepare what you want to eat.

If you find it hard to make friends, cooking can help you connect with others as you sit down together and enjoy the food that you have made.

Knowing how to cook helps you to be more independent when you grow up.

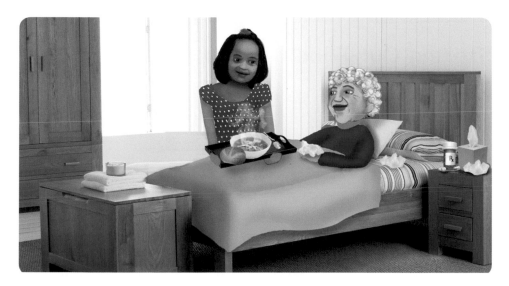

Cooking is also a skill that allows you to help people who are unable to provide for themselves to feel good and strong.

Chapter 2
Keeping Safe

The Keeping Safe chapter teaches you how to protect yourself in the kitchen. Cooking is fun and enjoyable but there are important rules and guidelines to remember every time you cook, to make sure you don't hurt yourself.

It's best to take a few moments each time to read over the following pages to help you keep safe in the kitchen.

Storing Our Food

After shopping in the supermarket it can be confusing to know where to put all the food that we buy when we come home.

Every food item has a **shelf life**. This means an amount of time that the food can be kept at home before it turns bad and becomes unsafe to eat.

Every ingredient has a different shelf life and we can find out what that is by looking at the packaging. For each item there is a **best before** or **use by** date that is written either on the top, side or bottom of the package. This date tells us how long we have left to eat that food. It is important to regularly check the dates on food packages to keep safe during food preparation.

Food needs to be stored in the correct place to help it to stay fresh for as long as possible.

Spoiled is what we call food that hasn't been eaten by the best before or use by date, or has not been kept in the right place and is not safe to eat.

Frozen foods must be the first items to put away when you come home from the supermarket to make sure they don't melt and spoil. Ice cream and frozen vegetables are examples of frozen foods and they must be stored inside a freezer to keep them fresh.

Chicken, meat and fish must be kept cold at all times. They need to be kept on the bottom shelf in the fridge. This is the coolest part of the fridge.

Uncooked chicken and meat is called **raw** and this type of food is packaged carefully to stop liquid from leaking out.

To keep safe, packages in the fridge should either rest on top of kitchen paper or be placed inside a plastic bowl to make sure the juices don't spoil other foods.

Storing times for raw and cooked chicken or meat are very important. Understanding the Keeping Safe rules can prevent illness and sickness.

Raw chicken, meat and fish can be kept for up to 2 days in the fridge. After that time it must be cooked or frozen.

Cooked chicken, meat and fish must be kept in the fridge and can be eaten for up to 4 days from when it was prepared.

If you want to reheat cooked chicken or meat, you should do this once only, and you must make sure it is piping hot before you eat it.

Eggs and milk are stored inside the door of the fridge.

Some fruit and vegetables are kept in the fridge to prevent them from going soft.

Others are able to stay fresh out of the fridge and they can be kept in a fruit bowl. Bananas make other fruit spoil faster so it's important to keep them separate.

Foods that don't need to be kept in the fridge are called cupboard ingredients and they have a longer shelf life. Olive oil, dry pasta and tinned tuna are examples of cupboard ingredients.

Food Preparation

Food can also spoil even if it is still fresh. It must be handled with care and attention at all times to prevent cross-contamination. This means that fresh food has been in contact with either uncooked chicken or meat, or perhaps it was handled with dirty hands or equipment. When this happens, bacteria can pass onto the fresh food, making it unsafe to eat.

Over the coming pages you will learn the rules of the kitchen that are there to help you keep safe. You will find out what to do and what not to do when learning how to cook.

These rules are in place to help you keep safe and prevent you or those eating your food from becoming unwell.

Let's take a closer look at the following possible dangers in the kitchen:

Raw chicken has bacteria inside it that only disappears when the chicken is fully cooked. Because of this, it must be prepared separately from all other ingredients, especially ones that can be eaten raw — for example, as salad ingredients such as cucumbers and tomatoes.

To help you keep safe, have two different colour-coded chopping boards in the kitchen as a reminder.

Kitchen equipment needs to be cleaned as quickly as possible after use. Dirty equipment is much harder to clean the longer it is left, and it also allows bacteria to grow on the old scraps of food.

Certain food is kept in a fridge because it needs to be in a cool environment in order to have a longer shelf life. The blue arrows show you how cool air circulates around the food to keep it at a safe temperature.

If the fridge is packed with food, the cool air cannot circulate properly. This causes the food to spoil much more quickly.

Kitchen towels and oven gloves are used all the time in the kitchen. Towels are used for drying our hands and wiping up spillages. Oven gloves protect our hands and wrists when we are carrying hot food. Kitchen towels, cloths and oven gloves become dirty very quickly so they should be changed often and washed in the washing machine at a high temperature.

The rubbish bin is filled with old or raw food scraps and packaging. The bag must be changed as soon as it is full. Hands must be washed well with soap and hot water every time we touch the rubbish bin.

Dos and Don'ts Checklist in the Kitchen

Here is list of health and safety guidelines to protect you as you cook and to make sure you have a safe and enjoyable experience in the kitchen.

 · · · · · · ·

Do tie long hair back securely at all times.

Don't leave it loose because hair will get in your food.

 · · · · · · ·

Do wear an apron securely fastened at the back.

Don't cook without protecting your clothing, because food spillages can stain.

Do wash your hands thoroughly with hot water and soap before cooking and after touching raw chicken, meat, fish or eggs.

Don't encourage cross-contamination in the kitchen.

Do pay careful attention to what you need to do at all times.

Don't let distraction cause accidents.

Do keep your kitchen tidy by clearing up as you go along.

Don't leave clean-up to the end as it can be tiring and messy.

Do wash your
equipment with
hot soapy water.

Don't leave it dirty to
spread harmful bacteria
to the food we eat.

Do ask for help if
you feel unsure.

Don't try to work out
what to do alone, you
may hurt yourself
by accident.

Do pay attention
to the time when
you are cooking.

Don't guess how long
food should be cooked
for or it won't turn
out as it should.

Chapter 3

Getting Started

Equipment

Saucepan

Colander

Soup ladle

Kettle

These pieces are used for boiling and serving liquids cooked on the hob.

Oven

Baking tray with rack

Baking tray

Round cake tin

Loaf tin

Wire rack

These pieces are used for baking and roasting food in the oven.

Frying pan

Flat spatula

Rounded slotted spatula

These pieces are used when frying different ingredients.

Knife

Vegetable chopping board

Meat cutting board

Peeler

Grater

These pieces are used to prepare food in different ways for all types of cooking.

Measuring cups

Measuring spoons

Mixing bowl

Metal spoon

Wooden spoon

Hand whisk

Electric whisk

Baking paper

Sieve

Cupcake case

Ice cream scoop

Basting brush

These pieces are used to prepare or serve different ingredients that are baked in the oven.

Timer

Kitchen towel

Oven gloves

Cling film

Tin foil

These pieces are used constantly in the kitchen for different types of food preparation.

Icon and Skill Glossary

The Icon and Skill Glossary lists the different kinds of techniques that are used when cooking in the kitchen. To help you learn how to do them, each skill is represented by an icon and explained with step-by-step instructions.

While cooking, if you need to refresh your mind about what to do, use the icon to come back to this glossary and check the correct instructions again. The icons are colour-coded to help you match them quickly.

Remember it is always better to stop and take the time to check again in order to keep safe in the kitchen!

Knife Icon and Skill

Knife Icon

Care and attention must be paid at all times when holding a knife.

The sharp part of the knife is called the blade. When carrying a knife at any time the blade must be pointing down towards the floor.

The knife must always be cutting in the direction of north to south ↕ from where you are standing so that you can see the blade at all times, never east to west ↔.

When chopping, hold the vegetable in a secure grip in a claw-like manner and keep your fingers tucked in, away from the blade. Use the middle part of the blade, not the point, to cut into the food.

When chopping vegetables for a soup, try to keep the pieces the same thickness to make sure they cook evenly.

Remember, work slowly.

Peeling Icon and Skill

 A peeler may not look as dangerous as a knife but it still has a very sharp blade.

Care and attention must be paid at all times while using a peeler.

Peeling Icon There are two ways to peel a fruit or vegetable.

1. Lay the vegetable down on a chopping board and, while holding one end, gradually peel the skin from the vegetable – this time going in the east to west direction ↔.

2. Hold the vegetable in one hand in a claw–like manner, keeping your fingers tucked in away from the blade.

Choose whichever method is most comfortable for you.

Remember, work slowly.

Grating Icon and Skill

Grating Icon

The different sized holes on a grater are as sharp as a knife, so careful attention must be paid at all times.

Use the regular-sized grating holes unless a recipe specifically calls for fine grating.

Hold the grater securely at the top so that it is stable against a chopping board.

When grating cheese or a vegetable, hold securely making sure to leave a space between your finger tips and the grater. Start at the top and work your way down, then up to the top and back down again.

When you have grated almost all the food, usually a lump remains and it is difficult to keep fingers away from the grater.

Place the food lump that is left in the middle of your hand and press the food and your flat hand against the grater. Continue to work up and down, keeping your hand flat at all times. You will be able to carry on working until all the food is grated.

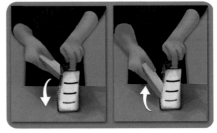

Hand Mixing Icon and Skill

Hand Mixing Icon

When mixing by hand, one hand must hold the side of the bowl at all times so you can keep control with your mixing hand.

Start off by using the claw technique to combine all the ingredients: spread the fingers out away from each other, bending each finger downward to create a hand grab and rest the weight of your hand on your fingertips. Then scoop your fingers together and scrape them around the bowl to bring in any extra ingredients that are stuck to the side.

If it is easier, turn the bowl while scooping round.

To remove dough stuck to your hand, take a small handful of extra flour in your other hand and rub your hands together – this will remove the stuck dough.

Kneading Icon and Skill

Kneading Icon

Kneading dough is an important part of bread baking as it helps to activate the yeast, the ingredient that makes the dough rise.

The kneading process is performed in three steps, which are repeated over and over again:

1. Lift the dough up from the back and fold it over towards you.

2. Using the ball of your hand, press sharply into the dough and push it away from you.

3. Lift the dough up from the back again, and fold it over towards you.

Turn the dough round as you work it and build up a smooth rhythm.

Repeat the process until the dough feels softer and bounces back if you poke your finger in it. This can take about 2–5 minutes.

Wooden Spoon Mixing Icon and Skill

Wooden Spoon Mixing Icon

Mixing with a wooden spoon is a great way to beat ingredients together to create a creamy and fluffy batter for cake baking.

For a creamy batter, follow a three-step process:

1. Dip the spoon in and under the batter.

2. Bring the spoon out of the batter.

3. Turn over and back into the batter.

The under-over-under technique helps to blend all the ingredients together, stopping any from getting stuck at the bottom. Work quickly with a strong arm.

It's usual for a mixture to look lumpy and grainy before it becomes smooth and creamy.

Metal Spoon Mixing Icon and Skill

Metal Spoon Mixing Icon

Mixing with a metal spoon is important for the last part of cake baking when the flour is combined with the creamy batter. The ingredients need to be combined very gently, with as little mixing as possible. A metal spoon has a thin edge that will not overwork the mixture, keeping it light, fluffy and airy – a perfect batter for baking.

Follow the three-step under-over-under technique:

1. Dip the spoon in and under the batter.

2. Bring the spoon out of the batter.

3. Turn the spoon over and put it back into the batter.

Work gently until all the ingredients are combined.

Cracking an Egg Icon and Skill

Cracking an egg can be messy if the egg is not held correctly.

This three-step process will help you to avoid spills:

Cracking an Egg Icon

1. Tap the middle of the egg against the side of a mixing bowl.

2. Bring the egg over to the middle of the bowl.

3. Hold the egg in both hands with both thumbs on each side of the new crack in the egg. At the same time, pull each side away from the other and allow the egg to pour into the bowl.

Sometimes egg shell also falls into the bowl and it can be hard to get it out. Simply take one half of the egg shell and use it as a scoop to pick out the shell – the shell pieces will connect immediately and your egg will be shell free!

Hand Whisking Icon and Skill

Hand Whisking Icon

A hand whisk is used when blending ingredients that need added air – a process called 'whisking' or 'whipping'. Whisks are used to whip cream or eggs, for example.

The whisk must move round and round and in and out of the batter, touching the base of the bowl as it goes inside, creating a tap tap tap sound.

Electric Whisk Icon and Skill

Electric Whisk Icon

An electric whisk is best used when mixtures or creams take longer to prepare. After a while, using a hand whisk would be tiring.

An electric whisk needs to be plugged into an electricity point. Take care not to use with wet hands.

Do not turn the whisk on until the blades are fully inside the mixture. Turn off the whisk while the blades are still inside the mixture – otherwise, the ingredients will fly out of the bowl!

Measuring Cups Icon and Skill

Measuring Cups Icon

Measuring ingredients correctly leads to successful cooking. Not taking care to measure slowly and carefully can lead to poor-tasting, unsuccessful cooking.

Follow these instructions carefully:

1. Take a heaped cup of the ingredient that needs to be measured.

2. With a regular knife, scrape slowly from the front of the cup to the back.

3. Push the excess ingredient away, leaving a flat, accurate measurement.

Measuring Spoons Icon and Skill

Measuring Spoons Icon

Measuring spoons require the same technique as cups.

Follow these instructions carefully:

1. Take a heaped spoon of the ingredient that needs to be measured.

2. With a regular knife, scrape slowly from the front of the spoon to the back.

3. Push the excess ingredient away, leaving a flat, accurate measurement.

Heat Icon and Skill

Heat Icon

Recipes will explain how high a heat should be when boiling or frying ingredients. There are three levels of heat: low, medium and high.

Turning the knob on the oven will change the level of heat.

All gas or electric stoves turn on differently, so ask a grown-up helper to explain how to turn it on and off at home.

It is important to remember that electric and ceramic hotplates, as well as gas rings, remain hot after you have turned them off. Bear in mind that saucepan handles can also become quite hot.

Hot Food Icon and Skill

Hot Food Icon

When handling hot food, always wear oven gloves to protect your hands and wrists from burns.

Make sure the grip on the equipment is strong before lifting or moving it to another place.

Keep a distance from the food. Baking trays, saucepans or frying pans should not rest against the body in any way. Even when smelling the delicious food, keep your face at a safe distance.

Boiling Icon and Skill

Boiling Icon

Boiling water and the steam it releases can cause serious burns to the body.

Always keep a distance between your body and the saucepan when boiling ingredients. Never lean into the saucepan to have a look. Hot steam can be as dangerous as boiling water.

Care and attention must be paid at all times to make sure that your body is away from the flame on a gas hob, too.

A rolling boil occurs when large bubbles come from the bottom of the saucepan and rise quickly to the surface. Clouds of steam are visible and the rolling boil will make a noticeable sound against the saucepan as all the water is in full movement. This technique is generally used for preparing pasta, boiled potatoes and other vegetables.

A simmer will show small intermittent bubbles that give off a gentle steam. This technique is used to blend flavours and cook food gently.

Frying Icon and Skill

Frying Icon

Frying involves heating oil gently, then adding ingredients to the hot pan.

Extra special care and attention must be paid at all times. If ingredients are dropped into a pan too quickly, they can cause hot oil to spit out of the frying pan.

One hand must remain on the handle at all times while mixing, flipping or frying food. Hold onto the middle of the handle, to have a strong grip.

Carefully guide a spatula with your free hand, according to the instruction in the recipe.

Oven Icon and Skill

Oven Icon

Oven gloves must be worn at all times when taking food in and out of the oven. Before removing cooked food, check there is a safe place ready to put it when it comes out of the oven.

Stand back when opening the door, the oven is very hot and a gust of hot air will immediately be released when the door opens. Keep safe and stand back.

Remember, ask a grown-up helper if you feel unsure.

Timing Icon and Skill

Timing Icon

Simply turn the dial on the timer to the time written in the recipe, and when the time is up it will buzz loudly. If you have a digital timer, ask a grown-up helper to show you how to set it.

Follow the timing instructions in every recipe carefully to make sure the food is cooked for the right amount of time.

Presentation Icon and Skill

Presentation Icon

Food may taste great and be cooked to perfection, but if it hasn't been presented nicely before it is served it won't be enjoyed as much as it could be.

It doesn't matter how simple the recipe is, food should always be 'dressed' beautifully, cleanly and neatly. Food presentation allows us to be really creative.

When you have finished cooking, take a moment to think about how to present your food before you serve it.

Recipe Layout and Explanation
Recipe Example

Cooking is exciting but it is also a process that takes time and careful attention.

A cooking recipe is an important kitchen tool that explains how to make successful meals, using equipment and ingredients in the right way.

Written instructions and pictures explain what needs to be done, and rushing through or missing parts out will lead to an unsuccessful meal.

Even the most famous chefs in the world follow recipes to make sure the final dish comes out just right.

Learning how to read a recipe takes practice so don't worry if you find it difficult at the beginning. The more you try, the easier it will become.

Recipe Name

Each recipe is presented with a photograph of the finished meal and has the name of the dish at the top.

Skills used:

Preparation time:

Cooking time:

Yield:

There is also a short explanation describing what skills you will use, how long it will take to prepare and cook the recipe and what the yield is, which means how many portions this recipe will make.

The recipe is then divided into steps to make it easier to follow.

Step 1: Equipment ready

Step 2: Ingredients ready

The first two steps are the same for each recipe. They are there so you have both the equipment and ingredients ready before you start. Completing these two steps makes it much easier to complete the instructions that follow.

The next steps in the recipe are known as the 'Method', which explains what skills are needed to prepare the ingredients. There will also be an icon reminding you how to use the right technique. If you are unsure of what to do, take a quick look back at the Icon and Skill Glossary. The Step headings below are examples only – they will be different in each recipe, depending on what you have to do.

Step 3: Start whisking

Step 4: Measuring and whisking

Step 5: Frying and flipping

This last step in every recipe gives suggestions for how the dish should be presented before it is served.

Step 6: Presentation

After cooking there is space at the end of each recipe for personal thoughts and comments to act as a reminder for next time. This will help you to develop tastes and record your likes and dislikes.

Your thoughts or comments

Remember: If you are unsure about what to do, you can remind yourself of the rules of the kitchen in Chapter 2, 'Keeping Safe', read over the Icon and Skills Glossary from Chapter 3, or simply ask a grown-up helper.

THE RECIPES

Level One Recipes

Level One is all about going back to basics and, ultimately, being brave.

Before starting to learn how to cook you must ask yourself one question: are you brave?

Tasting a variety of different and new foods can be challenging for some, but doing so allows you to find out what you really do or don't like. There may be ingredients you don't like the smell of but have never tasted, or foods that you have only seen in takeaway meals that you don't like the look of.

From here on you will be learning how to prepare and enjoy a wide variety of fresh, wholesome ingredients. You will be introduced to meals that can be produced from basic ingredients (also known as **staple foods**), such as flour, oil, salt, pepper and sugar. With a longer shelf life than most ingredients, they can be kept in store and be used in a variety of different ways. You will start to practise basic kitchen techniques that will allow you to bake your own bread, prepare ingredients from around the world and encourage your family and friends to enjoy mealtimes together.

This level will teach you how to think about food in a different way.

But you must know before you begin that it is not possible to be truly creative in the kitchen without being brave enough to try new foods first.

Peckish Pita Pieces

Sometimes, we just fancy something crunchy and tasty to eat in between meals. A bag of crisps is tasty but not so healthy for our bodies, so we can't eat them too often. Here is a delicious, healthy and crunchy alterative that is ready to eat from start to finish in 20 minutes. The best part is that, unlike a bag of crisps, Peckish Pita Pieces will keep you feeling fuller for much longer, giving you great brain power for school!

Skills used: knife, measuring spoons, oven, timing, heat, presentation

Preparation time: 10 minutes

Cooking time: 12 minutes

Yield: 4 people

Step 1: Equipment ready

Chopping board, knife, baking paper, baking tray, measuring spoons, 2 small bowls, basting brush, timer, metal spoon

Set the oven to 180 degrees Celsius (350 degrees Fahrenheit).

Step 2: Ingredients ready

1 wholemeal (wholewheat) pita

3 tablespoons olive oil

Pinch of coarse salt

½ tablespoon za'atar seasoning (available in all major supermarkets)

1 small tub of hummus

Step 3: Start chopping

Lay the pita on the chopping board and carefully cut the pita in half. Then cut each half in 2 to get 4 equal-sized triangles.

Gently tear each triangle in half at the fold to make 8 triangles altogether.

Step 4: Start measuring

Line the baking tray with baking paper, and lay the triangles on the baking paper.

Measure the olive oil into one of the small bowls.

Measure the za'atar seasoning into the other small bowl.

Step 5: Basting and roasting

Dip the basting brush into the olive oil and brush oil over each triangle.

Sprinkle a pinch of the salt and a little za'atar seasoning onto each triangle.

Ask a grown-up helper to help place the baking tray in the top of the oven.

Set the timer for 12 minutes.

After the timer beeps, remove the tray from the oven and leave the pita until it is cool to the touch.

Turn off the oven.

Step 6: Presentation

Empty the tub of hummus into a serving dish. To make the hummus look well displayed, draw the back of a metal spoon round and round over the surface.

Dunk the pita triangles, point down, into the hummus.

Your thoughts or comments

....

....

....

....

Baker's Bread

Making homemade bread may seem complicated, but if you follow these steps slowly and carefully you will see how simple it is. Understanding how to produce a loaf of bread in 1 hour with basic cupboard ingredients is very exciting and will allow you to provide a staple food at any time for all your family and friends.

Step 1: Equipment ready

Measuring cups, 2 mixing bowls, measuring spoons, loaf tin lightly sprayed with cooking oil, a glass, fork, cling film, basting brush, timer, knife

Set the oven to 200 degrees Celsius (400 degrees Fahrenheit).

Step 2: Ingredients ready

1½ cups wholemeal (wholewheat) flour

1 cup strong white bread flour + 1 extra cup white bread flour in a separate bowl for kneading

2 tablespoons golden brown sugar

1 heaped tablespoon dry yeast

¾ teaspoon coarse salt

¾ tablespoon vegetable oil

1 cup warm water (to measure the right temperature, use a ¼ cup of tap water with a ¼ cup of boiled water)

Cooking oil spray

1 egg mixed with a pinch of sugar, for basting

Step 3: Start measuring

Measure the wholemeal (wholewheat) flour and 1 cup of the strong white flour into a mixing bowl.

Measure the extra cup of strong white flour into another mixing bowl and put it aside.

Measure the sugar, yeast, salt, vegetable oil and water and add them to the first mixing bowl.

Step 4: Mixing

Using the claw technique, blend all the ingredients in the first mixing bowl together with your hand.

Sprinkle a large pinch of extra flour from the second bowl around the edges of the first bowl.

Scoop your hand around and scrape all the ingredients from the sides of the bowl so they are mixed in well.

Step 5: Start kneading

Keep bringing all the ingredients together.

Begin the three steps of kneading inside the bowl until a rough ball-shape forms.

Sprinkle some of the extra flour onto the kitchen work surface.

Remove your dough from the bowl and continue the three-step kneading technique on the kitchen work surface. Use a strong arm – be tough! Use little pinches of extra flour to stop the dough sticking, but not too much.

Keep kneading until the dough looks smooth and soft and springs back when you poke your finger in it (takes about 2 minutes).

Step 6: Shaping and rising

Shape the dough into a rectangle shape and put it straight into the loaf tin.

Crack the egg into a glass. Add a pinch of sugar and use a fork to beat the egg and sugar until it is an even consistency.

 Use the basting brush to baste some egg over the dough.

Lightly spray a piece of cling film with cooking oil spray and cover the dough securely.

Set the timer for 20 minutes and leave the dough to rise in a warm place.

Step 7: Baking

 Remove the cling film and use your knife to score 3 slashes lightly into the dough.

Baste with the egg mixture again.

Place the loaf tin containing the dough in the top of the oven.

Set the timer for 25 minutes.

Remove the loaf tin from the oven, and turn off the oven.

Turn the loaf of bread out of the tin when it is cool enough to touch.

Step 8: Presentation

Slice the loaf while it's warm, and serve with some butter.

Your thoughts or comments

....

....

....

....

Double Bedded Eggs

Eggs have many uses in baking and cooking. They bind ingredients together and help to make creamy cakes, custards and sauces. They are also delicious simply fried or boiled.

Step 1: Equipment ready

Regular cutlery knife, frying pan, flat spatula, small bowl, toaster

Step 2: Ingredients ready

Knob of butter for frying + extra knob for spreading on the toast

1 large egg

Pinch of coarse salt

Pinch of black pepper

2 slices of bread

1 slice of cheese

Step 3: Start frying

Turn on the hob to a medium heat.

Put the knob of butter in the frying pan and swirl it as it melts.

Crack the egg into the small bowl and add the salt and pepper.

Slowly lower the bowl over the frying pan and gently drop the egg in.

Step 4: Cooking and flipping

The clear part of the egg will turn white as it cooks. When it is completely white and slightly brown round the edges, slide the spatula under the egg yolk. Lift the egg and gently flip it over.

Leave the egg upside down for 5 seconds for a soft egg and 10–15 seconds for a well-cooked egg.

Turn off the hob.

While the egg cooks, put two slices of bread in the toaster.

Step 5: Presentation

Butter the 2 slices of toast and lay them on a plate.

Hold the frying pan carefully and slip the spatula under the egg. Lift the egg and place it on top of one of your slices of toast.

Lay a slice of cheese over the egg. Place the other slice of toast on top to complete the sandwich.

Your thoughts or comments

....

....

....

....

Cheesy Popeye Pancakes

Pancakes are fun to make and you will feel a great sense of achievement when they are ready to eat. Savoury pancakes are a fabulous lunch or teatime treat that all the family can enjoy. The spinach and wholemeal (wholewheat) flour in Cheesy Popeye Pancakes means they are tasty and nutritious.

> **Skills used:** measuring cups, measuring spoons, grating, hand whisking, heat, frying, hot food, presentation
>
> **Preparation time:** 10 minutes
>
> **Cooking time:** 10 minutes
>
> **Yield:** approximately 8 pancakes

Step 1: Equipment ready

Measuring spoons, measuring cups, mixing bowl, grater, sieve, metal spoon, hand whisk, frying pan, ice cream scoop, flat spatula

Step 2: Ingredients ready

1 cup wholemeal (wholewheat) flour

2 teaspoons baking powder

½ teaspoon coarse salt

Pinch of black pepper

Pinch of ground nutmeg

1 cup milk

1 egg

1 cup grated red Leicester cheese

2 cubes of frozen spinach, defrosted

4 tablespoons olive oil

Step 3: Measuring and whisking

Measure out the flour, baking powder, salt, pepper and nutmeg, and add them to the mixing bowl.

Make a little well in the middle of the mixture and add the milk, egg and ¾ of the cup of grated cheese. This is your batter.

Put the spinach in the sieve and press it with the back of the spoon to remove all the liquid.

Now add the spinach to the batter in the mixing bowl.

Whisk until almost smooth — it's okay to have a few lumps!

Step 4: Frying and flipping

Turn on the hob to a medium heat. Drizzle 1 tablespoon of olive oil into the frying pan and place on the hob.

Scoop out the batter using the ice cream scoop and gently drop two rounds into the hot frying pan, keeping space between the two. Keep focused on the pancakes and wait for little bubbles to appear and begin to pop.

Sprinkle a little of the remaining grated cheese on the top.

Slide the spatula under the pancake and gently flip it, taking care not to spatter the other pancake in the pan.
Do the same with the second pancake.

Cook each pancake for another 30 seconds and then transfer them from the pan onto a plate.

Add another tablespoon of oil to the pan, and repeat until all the pancakes are cooked.

Turn off the hob.

Step 5: Presentation

Pancakes look wonderful stacked on top of each other. It is okay if they are not all the same shape – they look even better when they are a little different.

Your thoughts or comments

....

....

....

....

Loaded Potatoes

The potato comes from the carbohydrate food group and is one of the world's cheapest food crops. It contains lots of vitamins and minerals that help keep our body strong and energised. Simply baking them in the right way provides a delicious warming meal.

Step 1: Equipment ready

Baking tray with wire rack, regular cutlery fork, measuring spoons, timer, kitchen towel

Set the oven to 220 degrees Celsius (425 Fahrenheit).

Step 2: Ingredients ready

2 large white potatoes, washed and dried

1 tablespoon olive oil

For the filling (choose any of the following)

Butter

Grated cheese

Baked beans

Tuna mayonnaise

Sour cream with chopped chives

Step 3: Preparation for baking

Prick the potatoes in three places with the fork.

Rub the potatoes with the olive oil.

Place the potatoes side by side on the wire rack on top of the baking tray.

Step 4: Baking

Place the baking tray at the top of the oven.

Set the timer for 1 hour.

When the timer beeps, remove the tray from the oven. **Ask a grown-up helper** if you need help to do this.

Turn off the hob.

Step 5: Presentation

Leave the potatoes to cool for a few minutes and use the kitchen towel to rest your hand over the hot potato as you cut it.

Baked potatoes are delicious simply served with butter. Alternatively, you can choose any of the other filling suggestions.

Your thoughts or comments

••

••

••

••

Minestrone Madness

Preparing a vegetable soup is a great way of using up root vegetables that have been left in the fridge, rather than throwing them away. Perhaps they are not fit for a salad but they are good enough to make a delicious, healthy soup. Minestrone soup can be a wonderful accompaniment to lunch or dinner, or a meal in itself served with a warm bread roll.

> **Skills used:** knife, peeling, heat, frying, boiling, timing, hot food, presentation
>
> **Preparation time:** 20 minutes
>
> **Cooking time:** 30 minutes
>
> **Yield:** 6 people

Step 1: Equipment ready

Peeler, knife, chopping board, measuring cups, measuring spoons, large saucepan with lid, timer, rounded spatula, soup ladle, grater

Step 2: Ingredients ready

1 onion, peeled, cut in half and sliced

2 carrots, peeled and chopped into equal round slices

2 sticks of celery + leaves, washed and chopped into small slices

1 courgette (zucchini), washed and chopped into cubes

1 small leek, sliced

½ cup frozen peas

½ cup sliced white cabbage

Handful of cubed pumpkin

2 tablespoons olive oil

2 teaspoons coarse salt

2 teaspoons vegetable stock powder

Pinch of black pepper

¼ cup barley

7 cups cold water

6 crusty rolls

½ cup grated Parmesan cheese

Handful of croutons to taste

Step 3: Preparing the soup mix

Put all the peeled and chopped vegetables into the saucepan and add the olive oil.

Turn on the hob to a medium heat. Put the saucepan on the hob and when the vegetables start to sizzle, gently mix them around in the oil using the spatula.

Set the timer for 2 minutes. Cover the saucepan with a lid and let the vegetables gently cook, or **sweat**, for a few minutes to soften them and release their liquid, which adds more flavour to the broth.

Remove the saucepan lid and add the salt, stock powder, pepper, barley and water.

Step 4: Boiling the soup

Cover the saucepan again, set the timer for 30 minutes and simmer the soup (still on a medium heat).

When the timer beeps, turn off the hob, remove the saucepan lid and leave the soup to cool slightly for a few minutes.

Step 5: Presentation

Using a soup ladle, carefully pour 2 ladles of soup into each serving bowl.

Be sure to fill each ladle so it contains both liquid and vegetables.

Sprinkle the soup with grated Parmesan cheese and chunky croutons or serve it with a hot, crusty bread roll.

Your thoughts or comments

....

....

....

....

Farfallino Pasta

Italy is famous for its pasta, and an important part of Italian life takes place in the kitchen, especially around mealtimes with family and friends. Italy is therefore a great country to copy when you want to encourage your family to sit down together and enjoy a meal.

Italy's reputation for cooking is built upon the quick and easy preparation of delicious and nutritious foods. In recent times, pasta and pizza have found their way into the fast food diet and therefore are thought of as a fattening food choice. However, if prepared the authentic Italian way with wholesome ingredients, pasta is another staple food that can successfully contribute to a healthy, balanced diet.

Step 1: Equipment ready

Large saucepan with lid, timer, frying pan, colander, grater, knife, chopping board, rounded spatula, measuring spoons

Step 2: Ingredients ready

For the pasta

12 cups water

1½ tablespoons coarse salt

250g (9oz) of good quality Farfalla pasta

For the pasta sauce

1 tablespoon olive oil

½ red onion, cut into cubes

1 garlic clove, sliced

400g (14oz) tin of good quality Italian chopped tomatoes + ½ of the tin refilled with water

2 tablespoons tomato purée

¾ teaspoon coarse salt

2 teaspoons golden brown sugar

Pinch of black pepper

Small pinch of cayenne pepper

Handful of fresh basil leaves, torn

1 ball of fresh mozzarella cheese

Grated Parmesan cheese, to taste

Step 3: Start boiling

Put the water in the saucepan and cover with a lid.

Turn on the hob to high and put the saucepan on the hob.

When the water boils, take off the lid, add the salt and then add the pasta. Leave the saucepan uncovered.

Set the timer and boil the pasta for 1 minute less than it says on the packet instruction. Stir the pasta occasionally during cooking.

Step 4: Prepare the sauce

While the pasta is cooking, put the olive oil in the frying pan.

Turn on the hob under the frying pan to a medium heat.

Add the onion and garlic to the frying pan and fry gently for 1 minute until the onions become transparent.

Add the tin of tomatoes and water, tomato purée, salt, brown sugar, black pepper, cayenne pepper and basil leaves. Stir everything around so it is well mixed.

Turn the heat down a little and simmer the sauce for a few minutes.

Step 5: Drain the pasta

When the timer beeps, turn off the hob under the pasta.

Put the colander in the sink and pour the water and the pasta from the saucepan into the colander. **Ask a grown-up helper** if you need help to do this.

Set the drained pasta aside for a few minutes.

Step 6: Combine the pasta and the sauce

Tear the ball of mozzarella into pieces and add it to the bubbling sauce on the hob.

Add some Parmesan cheese to the sauce and stir it around.

Carefully add the pasta to the bubbling sauce. **Ask a grown-up helper** if you need help to do this. Slowly mix with the spatula to combine the sauce with the pasta.

Turn off the hob.

Step 7: Presentation

Using your spatula, put the pasta and creamy tomato sauce onto plates and sprinkle with some extra grated Parmesan cheese.

Your thoughts or comments

....

....

....

....

Fruit Mountain

Chopping fruit for a fruit salad makes eating fruit that much more enjoyable. The different flavours of all the fruits combined can be refreshing on a hot summer's day and this is a healthy, naturally sweet and light dessert at the end of a filling meal.

Step 1: Equipment ready

Knife, chopping board, mixing bowl, metal spoon, small spoon

Step 2: Ingredients ready

1 ripe, sweet–smelling melon

Bunch of black
seedless grapes

2 red apples

1 passion fruit

2 kiwi fruit

Handful of strawberries

Handful of blueberries

Juice of 1 orange

Step 3: Fruit preparation

Melon

Hold the melon securely and cut it in half.

Scoop out the seeds.

Turn the halves flesh–side down on the chopping board.

Cut each half into 3 pieces lengthwise.

Turn each piece over and run the knife along the melon just above the skin to remove the flesh.

Chop the flesh into chunks and add them to the mixing bowl.

Grapes

Wash the grapes, remove them from the stalk and add them to the mixing bowl.

Apples

Cut round the apple, holding onto the top next to the stalk. Try to avoid cutting into the core.

Slice and cube the apple pieces, then rinse them gently under the tap to remove any dirt, pat dry and add them to the mixing bowl.

Kiwi fruit

Peel the skin, wash and pat dry.

Slice them into equal-sized pieces, and add them to the mixing bowl.

Strawberries

Put the strawberries in a colander and wash them thoroughly.

Dry them gently with kitchen paper, then either pull off the stems or slice them off with a knife, and add the strawberries to the mixing bowl.

Blueberries

Wash the blueberries, pat dry, and add to the mixing bowl.

Step 4: Mixing

Add all the prepared fruit to a mixing bowl and gently mix using a metal spoon.

Cut an orange in half and squeeze the juice into the bowl.

Step 5: Presentation

Serve in a pretty glass or ceramic dish.

Top with passion fruit seeds, scooped out of the passion fruit with a small spoon.

Your thoughts or comments

....

....

....

....

Sticky Chocolate Cornflakes

Chocolate cornflakes are the ultimate party food. This all-time favourite treat is made healthier through the use of dark chocolate, which is richer in fibre, iron, magnesium and other minerals in comparison to milk chocolate.

> **Skills used:** measuring spoons, heat, metal spoon mixing, measuring cups, presentation
>
> **Preparation time:** 20 minutes
>
> **Cooking time:** 3 minutes
>
> **Yield:** 8–10 cases

Step 1: Equipment ready

Large saucepan, measuring cups, measuring spoons, metal spoon, 10 cupcake cases or cupcake tin, 2 metal teaspoons

Step 2: Ingredients ready

¼ cup butter

5 tablespoons golden syrup

½ cup dark chocolate chips

¼ cup cocoa

3 cups cornflakes

Hundreds and thousands for decoration (if you like)

Step 3: Melt the chocolate

Put the butter, golden syrup, chocolate and cocoa in a saucepan.

Turn on the hob to a low heat. Put the saucepan on the hob and gradually stir the mixture with a metal spoon until everything is melted and combined.

Step 4: Coat the cornflakes

Turn off the hob.

Add the cornflakes and mix them in gently so as not to break them up too much. Keep mixing until they are almost coated.

Step 5: Fill the cupcake cases

Lay out the cupcake cases (or use a cupcake tin if you have one).

Using one of the metal teaspoons, scoop up some of the cornflakes and use the second teaspoon to scrape off the mixture into the cases.

Top up each case until they are all nicely full.

Put the cupcakes in the fridge, uncovered, for 30 minutes to set. If you want to decorate them (see the Presentation step below) do this first.

Step 6: Presentation

If you like, sprinkle hundreds and thousands over the top of each cupcake before putting them in the fridge to set.

Your thoughts or comments

....

....

....

....

Aunty Deb's Choc Chunk Cookies

Chunky, wholemeal (wholewheat), crunchy but soft chocolate chip cookies...nothing else needs to be said!

Step 1: Equipment ready

Measuring cups, measuring spoons, mixing bowl, wooden spoon, baking tray, baking paper, timer, flat spatula, wire rack

Set the oven to 170 degrees Celsius (325 degrees Fahrenheit).

Step 2: Ingredients ready

1 egg

½ cup brown sugar

½ cup caster sugar

½ cup regular oil

1 teaspoon vanilla essence

½ teaspoon bicarbonate of soda

½ teaspoon salt

1½ cups wholemeal (wholewheat) flour

1 cup dark chocolate chips

Step 3: Start measuring and mixing

Crack the egg into the mixing bowl.

Measure the brown sugar, caster sugar and oil into to the mixing bowl and blend with the egg until smooth.

Add the vanilla essence, bicarbonate of soda, salt, flour and chocolate chips.

Mix with a wooden spoon until all the ingredients are combined and have formed a soft, dough-like mass.

Step 4: Preparing to bake

Place baking paper on the baking tray.

Using a tablespoon, measure heaped and rounded spoons of cookie dough and place them on the baking paper 2.5–5cm (1–2 inches) apart.

Step 5: Baking

Place the baking tray near the top of the oven and set the timer for 14 minutes.

When the timer beeps, remove the baking tray from the oven. **Ask a grown-up helper** if you need help to do this.

Turn off the oven.

Wait for the cookies to cool slightly, then using the spatula transfer them to a wire rack to cool completely.

Step 6: Presentation

These biscuits will most likely be eaten up by all the family before you've had a chance to remove them from the rack! If there are any left, they are delicious with a cup of hot cocoa.

Your thoughts or comments

....

....

....

....

Level Two Recipes

Level Two helps you to practise and develop all the skills learnt in Level One, while introducing you to new ingredients, textures and flavours.

The ingredients you now have in your kitchen cupboards will be used again to show you that, with a little imagination, you can keep using them in many different ways.

Fish will be introduced in Level Two. A member of the protein food group, fish is known as a superfood! It is packed with vitamins and minerals and is a big source of omega 3 fatty acids that keep your brain strong and focused.

Some people don't like the look or smell of fish and prefer not to eat it. The recipes in the coming pages will introduce you to mild types of fish that are easy to prepare.

Remember, be brave – you might find that you enjoy a food that you never thought about trying before!

As you progress through Level Two, you may feel ready to attempt certain techniques alone where you before have needed a grown-up helper – work slowly and see how you feel.

If you feel unsure at any time during the cooking process, always ask a grown-up helper.

Pizza: The Italiano

Pizza baking will allow you to practise all the skills you have learned in Level One.

It takes a little extra time and there are quite a few more steps, but if you work slowly and carefully it will be worth it in the end.

A large, hot pizza can be placed in the middle of any table and shared amongst family and friends. There is nothing more confidence-boosting than to be able to invite friends over to share a delicious-tasting pizza that you have skilfully prepared yourself.

Step 1: Equipment ready

Mixing bowl, small bowl, measuring cups, measuring spoons, wooden spoon, cling film, timer, rolling pin, grater, baking tray, knife

Step 2: Ingredients ready

For the dough

½ cup wholemeal (wholewheat) flour

1 cup strong white bread flour + ½ cup extra for kneading in a separate bowl

1 full teaspoon dried yeast

1½ teaspoons golden sugar

¾ teaspoons salt

½ tablespoon olive oil

¾ cup warm water (¼ boiled water and ½ cold water)

Cooking oil spray

For the pizza sauce

½ cup tomato purée

2 tablespoons water

½ teaspoon salt

1 teaspoon golden sugar

Pinch of dried oregano

1 cup grated hard cheese, such as Cheddar or Monterey Jack

½ cup grated hard mozzarella cheese

Step 3: Measuring and hand-mixing

Measure out the flour, yeast, golden sugar, salt, olive oil and water into the mixing bowl.

Using the hand–mixing technique, quickly mix the ingredients into a ball.

Sprinkle some extra flour around the sides of the bowl to scrape in all the dough.

Step 4: Kneading dough

Sprinkle a little extra flour on the kitchen work surface and knead the dough for 2 minutes.

Add a little more flour if needed, but not too much!

Roll the dough around in your hands to create a smooth ball.

Wash and dry your mixing bowl, then spray with a little cooking oil spray. Turn the dough in the oil and cover the bowl with cling film.

Step 5: Rising

Set the timer for 20 minutes and leave the dough to rise in a warm place.

Set the oven to 200 degrees Celsius (400 degrees Fahrenheit) and place your baking tray inside the oven to warm up.

Step 6: Making the pizza sauce

Measure the tomato purée, water, salt, sugar and oregano into the small bowl.

Blend the ingredients together with a wooden spoon and set aside.

Step 7: Rolling the dough

Sprinkle the kitchen work surface with a little flour and turn out the soft dough.

Lightly flour the rolling pin and roll the dough out into a circle or rectangle. Don't roll the dough too thinly. It should have an even thickness and be light and elastic.

Step 8: Baking the pizza

Take the hot baking tray out of the oven. **Ask a grown-up helper** if you need help to do this.

Cooking oil spray the baking tray and carefully place the pizza dough on it (**be careful not to touch the hot pizza tray**). Reshape the dough with your hands if necessary.

Using the wooden spoon, smear the pizza sauce round and round the dough, starting from the middle and working outwards. Leave 2.5cm (1 inch) from the edge plain.

Sprinkle the cheeses over and add extra toppings of your choice.

Put the tray in the middle part of the oven and set the timer to 15 minutes.

When the timer beeps, take your pizza out of the oven. **Ask a grown-up helper** if you need help to do this.

Turn off the oven.

Step 9: Presentation

Use a pizza cutter, or ask a grown-up to help cut the pizza into slices, and enjoy with friends or family.

Your thoughts or comments

....

....

....

....

Creamy Scrambled Eggs with Smoked Salmon

Eggs have been used as an ingredient in different ways in Level One recipes. You have learned how to prepare and enjoy a simple fried egg and now you will learn how to prepare eggs by scrambling them. Scrambled eggs are soft and smooth and have a delicious creamy texture that goes very well with the salty taste of smoked salmon.

Chives are used here for the first time. This is a herb and it looks like a hollow blade of grass. You will also notice that it has a faint onion smell. This is because it is the smallest member of the onion family but its taste is milder than that of onions – an ideal topping for scrambled eggs on toast.

Step 1: Equipment ready

Mixing bowl, hand whisk, regular cutlery knife, measuring spoons, frying pan, large metal spoon, knife, chopping board

Step 2: Ingredients ready

6 large eggs

Pinch of coarse salt

Pinch of black pepper

2 teaspoons butter

2 tablespoons milk

2 heaped tablespoons cream cheese

Small pieces of smoked salmon

Small handful of fresh chives, chopped

Step 3: Hand-whisking and frying

Crack the eggs into a mixing bowl.

Add a pinch of salt and a pinch of black pepper to the mixing bowl.

Start hand-whisking the eggs until they are well beaten.

Turn on the hob to medium and melt the butter in the frying pan over the heat until it starts to bubble.

Step 4: Scrambling eggs

Add the eggs to the pan and keep whisking them round and round.

Stop whisking and add the milk, then carry on whisking until the eggs and milk are combined.

As the eggs start to form, stop whisking and add the cream cheese. Continue whisking until the eggs are just set.

Turn off the hob.

Step 5: Presentation

Lay a slice of buttered toast on a plate. Place a large spoonful of egg on the toast and add some pieces of smoked salmon.

Top with another spoonful of egg and more pieces of smoked salmon.

Sprinkle the chives on top.

Your thoughts or comments

....

....

....

....

Quick Mushroom and Pea Risotto

Arborio rice is Italian rice that is famous for its deliciously creamy texture once cooked. It is a warming introduction to cooking rice that is a meal in itself or can act as a side dish to fried fish. Either way, it will leave you feeling fully satisfied!

Skills used: knife, boiling, measuring cups, measuring spoons, wooden spoon mixing, grating, timing, hot food, presentation

Preparation time: 10 minutes

Cooking time: 20 minutes

Yield: 4 people

Step 1: Equipment ready

Knife, chopping board, large saucepan with lid, measuring cups, measuring spoons, wooden spoon, grater, kettle, timer

Step 2: Ingredients ready

Knob of butter

2 tablespoons olive oil

1 onion, finely cut into cubes

6 large mushrooms, sliced

1½ cups Arborio rice, unwashed

¾ teaspoon coarse salt

Pinch of black pepper

2 tablespoons vegetable stock, dissolved in 4 cups boiling water in a jug or mixing bowl

¼ cup frozen peas

1 cup grated Parmesan cheese + extra shavings to serve

Step 3: Start frying in the saucepan

Turn on the hob to a medium heat. Put the butter and olive oil in the saucepan and place it on the hob.

When the butter has melted, add the onion and fry for about 1 minute until slightly brown.

Add the mushrooms and fry, turning them around in the onions.

Add the rice and turn it around in the mixture until the grains are glossy.

Step 4: Cooking the risotto

Add the salt, pepper and vegetable stock to the rice and mix in.

Cover the saucepan with a lid and set the timer for 15 minutes.

Cook on a medium heat, lifting the saucepan lid every few minutes to stir.

When the timer beeps, add the frozen peas and set the timer for another 3 minutes.

Mix in the grated Parmesan and turn off the hob.

Step 5: Presentation

Served the risotto heaped in a small bowl or on a plate, and top with Parmesan shavings.

Your thoughts or comments

....

....

....

....

Crispy Mac 'n' Cheese

Mac 'n' cheese is one of America's favourite dishes. It can be eaten as soon as the pasta is mixed with a creamy white sauce or it can be baked further in the oven to give it a crispy topping. However you prefer to eat yours, here is how to make it.

Step 1: Equipment ready

Large saucepan, colander, small saucepan, measuring cups, measuring spoons, hand whisk, rounded spatula, baking dish, timer, grater

If you want to give your macaroni a crispy topping, set the oven to 190 degrees Celsius (375 degrees Fahrenheit).

Step 2: Ingredients ready

For the pasta

12 cups water

1½ tablespoons coarse salt

250g (9oz) of good quality macaroni pasta

For the cream sauce

3 tablespoons butter

2 tablespoons wholemeal (wholewheat) flour

1 teaspoon dry mustard powder

2 cups full fat milk

1 cup grated Cheddar cheese

½ teaspoon coarse salt

½ cup grated Parmesan

1 tablespoon breadcrumbs

Step 3: Boiling the pasta

Put the water in the large saucepan. Turn the hob heat to high and bring the water to a rolling boil.

Add 1½ tablespoons salt.

Add the pasta, bring back to the boil and set the timer for 1 minute less than it says on the packet instruction.

Boil uncovered and stir occasionally with the spatula.

When the timer beeps, drain the pasta into a colander over the sink.

Turn off the hob.

Step 4: Making the cream sauce

While the pasta cooks turn on another hob ring to a medium–low heat.

Put the butter in the small saucepan and heat until melted and bubbling.

Add the flour and the mustard powder.

Whisk gently with a hand whisk until nicely combined and foamy.

As you whisk with one hand, gradually add a cup of milk with the other hand and keep whisking until combined and starting to thicken.

Gradually add the second cup of milk and then add the salt. Keep whisking until combined.

Leave the sauce to sit on a medium–low heat until it begins to bubble round the edges, then turn off the heat.

Add a handful of grated cheese and whisk in until melted and combined.

Add the cooked macaroni and mix in using the spatula until the pasta is well coated with sauce.

Step 5: Crisping the macaroni

The macaroni can be eaten at this point but if you would like to crisp it up, transfer it to the baking dish.

Sprinkle with half the grated Parmesan cheese then sprinkle with the fine breadcrumbs and top with a little more grated cheese.

Set the timer for 15 minutes and cook in the oven.

When the timer beeps, take the baking dish out of the oven. **Ask a grown-up** if you need help to do this.

Turn off the oven.

Step 6: Presentation

Before crisping in the oven, put the macaroni in a nice oven-to-table dish and serve as soon as it comes out the oven!

Your thoughts or comments

....

....

....

....

Lentil Soup with Cheesy Garlic Bread

Red lentils are seeds from legume plants and are packed with nutrients that improve your health and help you maintain a healthy, balanced weight.

When boiled together with seasonings and vegetables they create a creamy, warming soup that is wonderful on a cold winter's night.

Coupled with cheesy garlic bread, this recipe will give you the opportunity to practise your bread-baking skills and will teach you that bread dough can be adapted for different recipes. Once you become more skilful, explore your tastes and think about what kind of bread you would like to make.

Step 1: Equipment ready

Knife, chopping board, grater, sieve, measuring cups, measuring spoons, large saucepan with lid, soup ladle, rounded spatula, mixing bowl, loaf tin, a glass, timer, basting brush, cling film

Set the oven to 180 degrees Celsius (350 degrees Fahrenheit).

Step 2: Ingredients ready

For the soup

1 tablespoon olive oil

2 peeled and sliced onions

1 clove of garlic, thinly sliced

2 tomatoes, thinly sliced

¾ teaspoon turmeric

2 cups whole red lentils, rinsed in sieve until the water is clear

6 cups water

¾ tablespoon coarse salt

Pinch of black pepper

For the cheesy garlic bread

1 prepared recipe of Baker's Bread dough (see page 90, Steps 1–5)

1 tablespoon olive oil

1 garlic clove, finely grated

Pinch of coarse salt

Pinch of dried thyme

½ cup finely grated Parmesan cheese

Cooking oil spray

1 egg, cracked in a glass and mixed with a pinch of sugar, for basting

Step 3: Preparing the soup

Turn the hob to a medium heat. Put the olive oil in the saucepan and heat gently on the hob.

Carefully add the sliced onions and garlic and fry for 1 minute, mixing occasionally with the spatula.

Add the sliced tomatoes and mix them in.

Add the turmeric and lentils, and mix everything together.

Add the water, salt and pepper. Stir and then put the lid on the saucepan.

Set the timer for 20 minutes and leave to simmer and thicken.

When the timer beeps, turn off the heat and leave the soup to sit while you finish preparing the bread.

Step 4: Preparing and rolling the dough

After kneading the dough, lightly flour the kitchen work surface and roll the dough out into a long rectangle shape so that it is not too thick, approximately 1–2cm (½–1 inch).

Brush the dough with olive oil. Rub in the finely grated garlic and sprinkle with a little coarse salt and dried thyme.

Sprinkle the grated Parmesan over the dough.

With a longer side of the rectangle closer to you, gently pull this edge out towards you then roll it over making sure to keep the cheese inside the roll, and taking care not to push it out as you roll. Pulling the roll up towards you a little will allow you to roll the cheese inside the dough rather than push it out.

Continue rolling all the way until you have one long fat tube of dough with all the cheese tucked inside.

Step 5: Cutting the dough

Cut the tube into equal-sized pieces, approximately 2.5–5cm (1–2 inches) wide.

Spray the loaf tin lightly with cooking oil spray.

Lay the dough rolls cut side down in the loaf tin. Place them really close to each other – you will find that they join together while they rise and bake.

Step 6: Rising and baking

Baste the prepared dough with the egg wash.

Spray a piece of cling film with cooking oil spray. Use this to cover the dough.

Set the timer and leave the dough to rise in a warm place for 20 minutes.

When the timer beeps, baste the dough again with egg wash and put in the middle of the oven.

Set the timer and bake for 25 minutes. When the timer beeps, take the loaf tin out of the oven and turn off the oven.

Step 7: Presentation

Ladle the soup carefully into soup bowls and break off a piece of cheesy bread for each person to dip into their soup.

Your thoughts or comments

....

....

....

....

Ocean Fishcakes

Making tuna fishcakes is an easy introduction to cooking with fish and is a delicious way to enjoy tinned tuna, a store cupboard staple.

Step 1: Equipment ready

Knife, chopping board, small saucepan with lid, colander, electric whisk, measuring cups, measuring spoons, 2 mixing bowls, fork, plate, frying pan, timer, spatula, kitchen paper

Step 2: Ingredients ready

For the fishcakes

1 medium potato

¼ tablespoon + ¼ teaspoon coarse salt

2 x 200g (7oz) tins of tuna, drained and flaked with a fork in a bowl

2 tablespoons tomato ketchup

1 tablespoon mayonnaise

Pinch of black pepper

½ cup fine breadcrumbs

1 egg

1–2 teaspoons olive oil

2 tablespoons olive oil + a knob of butter to fry each batch

For the coating

¼ cup wholemeal (wholewheat) flour

Pinch of coarse salt

Pinch of black pepper

For the Thousand Island dressing

2 tablespoons mayonnaise

½ tablespoon tomato ketchup

Step 3: Prepare the mashed potato

Peel and chop the potato into chunks and cover with water in a saucepan.

Turn on the heat to high and bring the potato to a boil.

Add ¼ tablespoon of coarse salt to the water and cover the saucepan with a lid.

Reduce the heat to medium, set the timer and boil the potato for 15 minutes until soft.

Turn off the hob. While the potato is cooking, prepare the tuna mix.

Step 4: Measuring and mixing

Put the tuna in one of the mixing bowls. Measure out the ketchup, mayonnaise, ¼ teaspoon salt, pepper and breadcrumbs and add them to the tuna.

Crack the egg into the same bowl and combine the mixture with a fork.

In a separate bowl measure out the wholemeal (wholewheat) flour, a pinch of salt and pepper. Mix by hand to combine.

Step 5: Mash the potato

When ready, carefully drain the potatoes in a colander in the sink and return them to the hot saucepan.

Drizzle a little olive oil on top and whisk until smooth with the electric whisk.

Add the mashed potatoes to the tuna mix and combine well.

Step 6: Shape and fry the fishcakes

Fill a ¼ sized measuring cup with the fishcake mixture and pat it out onto the palm of your hand.

Flatten slightly and dip both sides into the flour mixture.

Put the prepared fishcakes on a plate ready to fry.

Heat 2 tablespoons of olive oil and a knob of butter on a medium heat in the frying pan and swirl around.

Add 5 fishcakes to the pan and set the timer for 2 minutes.

When the timer beeps, slide the spatula under each fishcake and gently turn over. Set the timer and fry for another minute, then remove from the pan and leave to rest on kitchen paper to absorb any excess oil.

Cook the remaining fishcakes in the same way.

Turn off the hob.

Step 7: Presentation

Mix the mayonnaise and ketchup together in small bowl and serve your Thousand Island dressing alongside warm or room-temperature fishcakes laid nicely on a plate.

Your thoughts or comments

....

....

....

....

Fish Fingers with Wild West Wedges

Fish and chips are an all-time British favourite dish. The downside is that when you buy fish and chips from a takeaway, they are usually loaded up with unwanted fat and salt. Try this tasty, healthy recipe at home instead — your friends and family will love it!

Step 1: Equipment ready

Measuring cups, measuring spoons, baking tray, timer, 3 small mixing bowls, large plate, frying pan, flat spatula, knife, chopping board, plate with scrunched kitchen paper

Set the oven to 200 degrees Celsius (400 degrees Fahrenheit).

Step 2: Ingredients ready

For the potato wedges

4 medium-sized white potatoes

4 tablespoons olive oil

2 pinches of coarse salt

2 pinches of black pepper

2 pinches of garlic powder

1 teaspoon sweet paprika

For the fish fingers

½ cup wholemeal (wholewheat) flour

1 egg

2 tablespoons vegetable oil

1 teaspoon fine salt

Pinch of garlic

Pinch of black pepper

1 cup golden breadcrumbs

1 large cod fillet cut into fingers

5 tablespoons vegetable oil for frying

Step 3: Preparing the potato wedges

Wash the potatoes.

Cut the potatoes in half and then into wedges. There is no need to peel them.

Put the olive oil, salt, black pepper, garlic powder and sweet paprika onto the baking tray and lightly mix with your finger tips.

Put the potato wedges on the baking tray and turn them over, coating them all over with the oil and seasoning.

Level the potatoes out and keep them flat on the tray.

Set the timer for 45 minutes and put the baking tray at the top of the oven.

Step 4: Preparing the fish fingers

Line up 3 small bowls.

Put the flour in the first bowl.

Crack the egg into the second bowl and add the olive oil, salt, garlic powder and black pepper. Whisk until combined.

Put the breadcrumbs in the third bowl.

Dip each fish finger one by one into the flour, then into the egg and finally into the breadcrumbs. Put the breaded fingers on a plate ready for frying.

Keep one hand for wet dipping and one hand for dry dipping – that way, you will keep fairly clean until the end.

Step 5: Frying and flipping

Turn the hob on to a medium heat and put the olive oil in the frying pan. Heat the oil until small bubbles appear, then very gently lower 5 fish fingers into the frying pan. Be careful not to drop them in or the hot oil will splash.

Allow the oil to come back to bubbling, leave the fish fingers for about 1 minute so they go golden in the oil. Then flip them over with the spatula, wait for the oil to bubble again, and cook for another minute.

When the fish fingers are golden all over, carefully remove them from the frying pan and lay them on the kitchen paper to cool.

Turn off the hob.

Step 6: Presentation

When the timer beeps and the wedges are ready, carefully remove them from the oven and turn off the oven.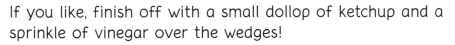

Using a spatula, place a pile of wedges together on each person's plate next to the fish fingers.

If you like, finish off with a small dollop of ketchup and a sprinkle of vinegar over the wedges!

Your thoughts or comments

....

....

....

....

Classic Victoria Sponge

Victoria Sponge was named after Britain's Queen Victoria (1818–1901), who would enjoy a daily slice with her afternoon tea. It is a classic first cake to make.

Step 1: Equipment ready

Kitchen paper, 2 round cake tins (20cm [8 inches] in diameter), baking paper, pencil, scissors, 2 mixing bowls, measuring cups, measuring spoons, sieve, wooden spoon, electric whisk, timer, cake spatula, metal spoon, cake stand

Set the oven to 180 degrees Celsius (350 degrees Fahrenheit).

Step 2: Ingredients ready

1 cup butter at room temperature + knob for greasing the cake tins

1 cup caster sugar

1 cup wholemeal (wholewheat) flour

2 teaspoons baking powder

2 tablespoons milk

4 large eggs at room temperature

½ cup cold whipping cream

4 tablespoons strawberry jam

Icing sugar

Step 3: Preparing the cake tins

Put a knob of butter on a piece of kitchen paper and rub the butter all the way around the two cake tins.

Put the cake tins on a sheet of baking paper and draw around them with a pencil.

Cut out the outlined circles and place one in each of the cake tins, with the pencil side down.

Step 4: Measuring and electric whisking

Put the butter and sugar in the mixing bowl and beat with the wooden spoon until creamy, fluffy and lighter in colour.

Sift the flour together with the baking powder into the butter and sugar mixture, then add the milk.

Crack the 4 eggs into the mixing bowl and whisk until fully combined and fluffy.

Step 5: Oven and timing

Divide the mixture equally between the two cake tins and flatten the top with the spatula.

Place near the bottom of the oven and set the timer for 25 minutes.

When the timer beeps, remove the cakes from the oven, turn off the oven, and leave the cakes to cool.

Step 6: Whisking cream

Put the cream in another mixing bowl and beat with the electric whisk until almost firm (wash the beaters first as they will be messy from the sponge mixture).

Step 7: Filling the cake

Turn the cakes out of the cake tins.

Lay one cake on a cake stand and spread the jam thickly over the surface but not too close to the edge.

Spread a thick layer of whipped cream over the jam, keeping it 2.5cm (1 inch) away from the edge of the cake.

Turn the second cake out of the tin and put it on top of the whipped cream, pressing down very gently.

Step 8: Presentation

Sprinkle evenly with icing sugar and serve with a lovely cup of tea.

Your thoughts or comments

....

....

....

....

Vanilla Ice Cream

Ice cream parlours churn their ice cream and blend it with different flavours and textures using special machinery, but there is no reason why vanilla ice cream can't be made at home.

   Once you are used to making this ice cream, pep it up a little by adding chocolate chips, or smashed chocolate cookies, fresh strawberries or chocolate mints. Whatever your taste, explore it — the choice is yours!

Step 1: Equipment ready

Mixing bowl, measuring cups, measuring spoons, electric whisk, cake spatula, ice cream box, ice cream scoop

Step 2: Ingredients ready

2 cups cold whipping cream

½ cup caster sugar

4 large fresh eggs

2 teaspoons vanilla essence

Cones or wafers or hundreds and thousands, for serving

Step 3: Start whisking the cream

Pour the whipping cream into a bowl and whisk on a high speed until almost firm.

Step 4: Measuring and whisking

Add the sugar, eggs (one at a time) and vanilla essence. Continue whipping until fully blended and thick.

Step 5: Freezing

Transfer the cream mixture, using a cake spatula, to an ice cream or plastic box.

Smooth the top, cover tightly and freeze overnight.

Step 6: Presentation

Take the ice cream out of the freezer and leave to soften slightly for a few moments.

Dip the ice cream scoop into a cup of hot water before scooping out balls of ice cream.

Serve in cones or individual cups with wafer biscuits or sprinkles.

Your thoughts or comments

....

....

....

....

Gooey Chocolate Brownies

Brownies are usually flat, square and very chocolatey. They are a cross between a cake and a cookie. Everyone has a brownie favourite and now it's time to explore yours. Here is a recipe for soft, chewy and utterly delicious brownies that will have your family and friends coming back for more!

Step 1: Equipment ready

Small saucepan, measuring cups, measuring spoons, mixing bowl, sieve, a glass, wooden spoon, metal spoon, hand whisk, cake spatula, square brownie baking tin (25 x 25 x 5cm [10 x 10 x 2 inches]), baking paper, timer

Set the oven for 180 degrees Celsius (350 degrees Fahrenheit).

Grease and line the baking tray with baking paper.

Step 2: Ingredients ready

½ cup butter

¾ cup caster sugar

½ cup dark brown sugar

1 cup dark chocolate chips

1 tablespoon golden syrup

1 teaspoon vanilla essence

2 eggs, cracked into a glass

¾ cup wholemeal (wholewheat) flour

2 tablespoons cocoa

1 teaspoon baking powder

Step 3: Start melting

Turn on the hob to a low heat. Put the butter, caster sugar, dark brown sugar, chocolate chips and golden syrup in the saucepan. Put the saucepan on the hob and stir the mixture gently with the wooden spoon until everything has melted. Remove from the heat to cool for a few minutes.

Step 4: Whisking

Add the vanilla essence to the chocolate mixture, then add the eggs and whisk until combined and smooth.

Step 5: Sifting and folding

Rest the sieve over your mixing bowl and then measure the flour, cocoa and baking powder into the sieve.

Hold the sieve in one hand and gently bang it back and forth against your other hand which stays still.

The flour mixture will simply fall through the sieve into the mixing bowl.

Add the flour mixture to the melted chocolate and fold in gently with a metal spoon.

Pour the mixture into the prepared baking tin and level the surface with the spatula.

Set the timer and bake near the bottom of the oven for 25 minutes.

When the timer beeps, take the brownies out of the oven and turn off the oven.

Step 6: Presentation

Enjoy the brownies warm, topped with a ball of melting Vanilla Ice Cream (see page 150).

Your thoughts or comments

....

....

....

....

Level Three Recipes

Level Three is the final stage of your first cookery course. Now your skills are developed, you can prepare vegetables, eggs and dough. You can bake, boil and present food in creative ways. Your confidence in the kitchen is growing and you are beginning to explore your food tastes and preferences.

As Level Three introduces you to chicken and meat, pay careful attention to the rules of the kitchen in order to keep safe. Always remind yourself of the health and safety instructions before you handle raw and cooked food.

Enjoy providing yourself and your family and friends with healthy and nutritious meals. Pat yourself on the back – you're doing an amazing job!

As for the earlier recipes, if you feel ready to attempt certain techniques alone where before you may have needed a grown-up helper, work slowly and see how you feel.

If you feel unsure at any time during the cooking process, always ask a grown-up helper.

Simply Perfect Roast Chicken with Basmati Rice

Many people believe that the only way to make delicious chicken is to season it or glaze it with sauces and marinades. That is simply not true.

Chicken has a delicious hearty, tasty flavour all of its own. The secret to bringing out the flavour of a whole chicken is to cook it in a small deep dish on a lower heat for a longer time.

This way, the natural flavours of the chicken produce delicious gravy which helps to soften the chicken that sits in it while it cooks through.

This dish is a winner every time and shows that very little needs to be done to enjoy a tasty and nutritious meal.

> **Skills used:** oven, measuring cups, measuring spoons, frying, boiling, hot food, presentation
>
> **Preparation time:** 8 minutes
>
> **Cooking time:** 2 hours
>
> **Yield:** 4–6 people

Step 1: Equipment ready

Roasting tin, small saucepan with lid, measuring cups, measuring spoons, sieve, rounded spatula, metal spoon, timer, knife, tin foil

Set the oven to 160 degrees Celsius (315 degrees Fahrenheit).

Step 2: Ingredients ready

1 medium to large whole roasting chicken

1 cup basmati rice

1 tablespoon olive oil

½ teaspoon coarse salt

2 cups water

Step 3: Start roasting

Place the chicken in a roasting tin and put it near the top of the oven.

Set the timer for 2 hours.

When the chicken is cooked, the juices from the chicken should run clear when pierced with a knife, and there should be no red in the juices.

Step 4: Boiling the rice

30 minutes before the chicken is finished, put the rice in a sieve.

Rinse the rice thoroughly under cold water until the water runs clear.

Turn on the hob to a medium heat. Put the olive oil in the saucepan and heat gently.

Add the rice and the salt and stir with the spatula until the grains become separate and glossy.

Add the water, turn the heat down to medium–low and cover the saucepan with a lid.

Set the timer for 18 minutes.

When the timer beeps, turn the hob off but leave the lid on the saucepan to let the rice steam and finish cooking.

Step 5: Removing the chicken

Ask a grown–up helper to help you take the chicken out of the oven very slowly – there will be gravy in the roasting tin too.

Turn off the oven.

Leave the chicken to cool slightly under some tin foil and ask your helper to carve the chicken.

Step 6: Presentation

Spoon some hot rice onto a plate and top with a piece of hot roast chicken and a spoonful of gravy.

Your thoughts or comments

....

....

....

....

Classic Chicken Noodle Soup

Chicken soup, nicknamed 'Kosher Penicillin', is a traditional Jewish food that is thought to be a universal healer. For example, chicken soup is thought to provide relief from common cold symptoms such as congestion and a sore throat.

When winter comes, boil up some chicken broth to share with your family, especially those who are not feeling well and need a warming boost.

Step 1: Equipment ready

Knife for chopping raw meat, meat chopping board, vegetable knife, vegetable chopping board, peeler, large saucepan with lid, small saucepan, bowl, wooden spoon, measuring cups, measuring spoons, kettle, rounded spatula, timer, knife and fork for cutting the cooked chicken, colander, kitchen paper, soup ladle, metal spoon

Step 2: Ingredients ready

1 small whole chicken, chopped into pieces

8 cups water

1 tablespoon coarse salt

1 bay leaf

1 large onion, peeled and cut in quarters

2 carrots, peeled and sliced

2 sticks of celery, washed and sliced + a handful of leaves

½ teaspoon turmeric

Large pinch of black pepper

1 small packet of egg noodles

Step 3: Prepare the soup

Turn on the hob to a medium heat. Place the chicken pieces in the large saucepan and add the water, salt and bay leaf. Cover the saucepan with a lid, and bring to the boil on the hob.

Turn off the hob and leave the saucepan to cool.

Using a metal spoon, take of the 'scum' that has settled at the top.

Use 4–5 sheets of kitchen paper to remove the fat that has also settled on the top. To do this, take hold of the corner of a sheet, and lay it over the soup for a few seconds. Now lift it up and put in the bowl. Repeat with the other sheets until there is no more fat in the saucepan. (When you have finished, you can just put the dirty sheets in the bin.)

Step 4: Boil the soup

Turn the hob back on to a medium heat, cover the saucepan and set the timer for 45 minutes.

Step 5: Prepare the vegetables

While the soup is cooking, prepare your vegetables using the techniques you have learned for washing, peeling and cutting.

Step 6: Swap the chicken with the vegetables

When the timer beeps, turn off the hob, carefully remove the saucepan lid and leave the liquid to cool for a few minutes.

Ask a grown-up helper to help you remove the chicken pieces, using the spatula, and carefully place them on a chopping board.

Using your spatula again, gently put the prepared vegetables into the soup without dropping them in.

Add the turmeric and black pepper.

Replace the saucepan lid, set the timer and simmer on a medium heat for 30 minutes.

Step 7: Shred the chicken

Shred the chicken away from the bone using a knife and fork. Throw away the bones and all the skin.

When the timer beeps, use your spatula to return the chicken pieces to the soup.

Reset the timer for a further 10 minutes.

Step 8: Prepare the noodles

Place the raw noodles in the medium saucepan. Boil the kettle and **carefully** pour the boiling water over the noodles (use enough water to cover them). Leave for a few minutes until the noodles are soft.

Stir the noodles around with a fork to prevent them from sticking together, and then drain them in a colander.

Turn off the hob.

Step 9: Presentation

With a fork add a portion of noodles to a bowl and carefully ladle the soup with vegetable and chicken pieces over the top.

Your thoughts or comments

....

....

....

....

Crunchy Chicken with Sweet and Sour Cabbage

Crispy Southern fried chicken is famous worldwide. Here is a crunchy oven-baked version that is less messy to prepare, better for you because it isn't fried...and simply delicious.

Step 1: Equipment ready

3 small bowls, measuring cups, measuring spoons, hand whisk, baking tray, timer, knife, chopping board, frying pan, rounded spatula

Set the oven to 180 degrees Celsius (350 degrees Fahrenheit).

Step 2: Ingredients ready

For the drumsticks

½ cup wholemeal (wholewheat) flour

1 egg

2 tablespoons vegetable oil

1 teaspoon fine salt

Pinch of garlic powder

Pinch of black pepper

1 cup golden breadcrumbs

4 chicken drumsticks, skin removed

Cooking oil spray

For the sweet and sour cabbage

2 tablespoons olive oil

1 onion, peeled and cut into cubes

2 tablespoons brown sugar

½ red cabbage, sliced

2 heaped tablespoons strawberry jam

2 tablespoons vinegar

2 tablespoons water

1½ teaspoons coarse salt

Pinch of black pepper

2 bay leaves

Step 3: Bread the chicken

Line up 3 small bowls.

Put the flour in the first bowl.

Crack the egg into the middle bowl. Add the vegetable oil, salt, garlic powder and black pepper, and whisk until combined.

Put the breadcrumbs in the third bowl.

Dip each drumstick, one by one, into the flour, then into the egg and finally into the breadcrumbs and put them directly on a baking tray. Remember, it's less messy if you keep one hand for wet dipping and one hand for dry dipping.

Spray the chicken with cooking oil spray and put it in the over near the top.

Set the timer for 55 minutes. When the timer beeps, check that the chicken is cooked by cutting into one of the drumsticks. The meat should come away easily from the bone and the juices from the chicken should run clear.

Turn off the oven.

Step 4: Prepare the cabbage

While the chicken is cooking, turn on the hob to a medium heat. Put the oil in the frying pan and heat gently.

Add the chopped onion and stir it around in the oil, then add the sugar and stir again.

Fry the onion for 1 minute, until caramelized – the sugar should have melted and begun bubbling with the onions.

Add the cabbage, jam, vinegar, water, salt, pepper and bay leaves.

Turn the heat to medium–low. Set the timer for 25 minutes and simmer the cabbage mixture until the timer beeps.

When the cabbage is cooked, turn off the hob.

Step 5: Presentation

Serve the cabbage on the same plate as the crunchy drumsticks.

Next time, prepare some basmati rice and serve all three together.

Your thoughts or comments

....

....

....

....

Creamy Chicken Sandwich

After a meal of freshly roasted chicken, sometimes there are pieces that haven't been eaten (called 'leftovers') that can be stored in the fridge. Here is a tasty suggestion for what to do with leftover chicken (or turkey, if you have it).

Step 1: Equipment ready

Knife, regular cutlery fork, chopping board, mixing bowl, measuring spoons, metal spoon

Step 2: Ingredients ready

Cold cooked chicken

3 tablespoons mayonnaise

1 teaspoon mustard

2 slices of wholemeal (wholewheat) bread

2 leaves of washed lettuce

1 cucumber, sliced

Step 3: Start shredding

Using the knife and fork, carefully strip the cooked chicken away from the bone.

Chop the chicken into small chunks and put in a mixing bowl.

Step 4: Measuring and mixing

Add the mayonnaise and mustard to the chicken and mix well with a metal spoon.

Step 5: Presentation

Spread a little mayonnaise on one slice of bread, then top with lettuce and a spoonful of the chicken mixture.

Place the sliced cucumbers on top of the chicken and then put on the second slice of bread.

Your thoughts or comments

....

....

....

....

The Ultimate Burger

A burger and chips takeaway is called fast food and it tastes great but unfortunately it doesn't offer your body any of its much-needed nutrition. A takeaway uses a great deal of salt, sugar and unnatural flavours to make it taste great.

Here is a burger recipe that can be made in your own kitchen using just three ingredients to prepare the beef. It's not only a treat but is good for your body too.

Step 1: Equipment ready

Mixing bowl, measuring cups, measuring spoons, frying pan, flat spatula, metal spoon, knife, chopping board

Step 2: Ingredients ready

500g minced beef

¼ teaspoon black pepper

½ teaspoon coarse salt

1 tablespoon olive oil

4 burger buns

Burger fillings of your choice, for example sliced tomatoes, onions, pickled cucumbers, lettuce, fried egg

Step 3: Season the meat

Put the mince in a mixing bowl and push the meat towards the sides making a small well in the middle.

Sprinkle the pepper and salt over the meat, then turn the meat and mix thoroughly with a metal spoon.

Step 4: Shape the burgers

Make 4 burger shapes using the ½ cup measuring cup.

Tap them out into your hand and flatten them to approximately 1cm (½ inch) thick.

Step 5: Frying and flipping

Turn on the hob to a medium heat.

Heat the olive oil in the frying pan and wait until it is really hot.

Carefully put the four burgers in the pan using the flat spatula and set the timer to cook on a medium–high heat for 4 minutes.

When the timer beeps, sprinkle each burger with a little coarse salt and pepper, flip the burger carefully with the spatula and fry for a further 4 minutes.

Turn off the hob.

Step 6: Presentation

Slice the burger buns in half, then put the burgers and toppings of your choice between each half. Enjoy!

Your thoughts or comments

....

....

....

....

Bolognese

Bolognese sauce is a thick, meat-based sauce that is mixed with pasta. Originating from the 18th century, this sauce was named after the town in Italy — Bologna — that created it. Traditionally, the sauce is stewed for a long time but here you will learn a quicker version that makes a tasty and hearty meal for you and your family.

Step 1: Equipment ready

Knife, chopping board, measuring cups, measuring spoons, large saucepan, timer, colander, frying pan, wooden spoon, two metal spoons, grater

Step 2: Ingredients ready

For the pasta

12 cups water

1½ tablespoons coarse salt

250g (9oz) tagliatelli pasta

For the bolognese sauce

2 tablespoons olive oil

1 red onion, peeled and cut into cubes

1 carrot, grated

500g minced beef

400g (14oz) tin of Italian chopped tomatoes

1 tablespoon tomato purée

2 teaspoons coarse salt

Very small pinch of cayenne pepper

Pinch of ground nutmeg

Step 3: Boil the pasta

Turn on the hob to a high heat. Pour the water into the large saucepan and bring the water to a rolling boil.

Add 1½ tablespoons of salt to the water. Add the tagliatelli pasta, bring back to the boil and set the timer for 1 minute less than it says on the packet instruction. Boil uncovered and stir occasionally.

When the timer beeps, drain the pasta into a colander in the sink and turn off the hob.

Step 4: Prepare the bolognese

Turn on the hob to a medium heat. Put the olive oil in the frying pan and heat gently on the hob.

Add the red onion and stir with a wooden spoon for a few moments.

Add the grated carrot and fry together with the onions.

Add the minced beef. Using the wooden spoon, keep breaking up the mince and stirring it until it is brown and all mixed in with the vegetables.

Add the chopped tomatoes, tomato purée, salt, cayenne pepper and nutmeg. Mix everything together well, cover and leave to simmer on a medium–low heat.

Set the timer for 15 minutes, then when it beeps, remove the saucepan from the heat and turn off the hob.

Step 5: Mix the pasta with the meat

Gently add the pasta to the meat and combine using two metal spoons to draw the pasta up and back into the sauce.

Step 6: Presentation

Using two metal spoons (or kitchen tongs if you have them), spoon the bolognese into a bowl.

Put an extra spoonful of meat over the top.

Your thoughts or comments

....

....

....

....

Honey–Roasted Turkey with Sweet Potato Mash

Turkey is traditionally served in the US and UK on Christmas Day, but preparing a whole turkey is a pretty daunting task for many people.

To make it more manageable, here is a smaller alternative that will have all your guests asking for more.

Step 1: Equipment ready

Roasting tin with wire rack, measuring spoons, large saucepan with lid, peeler, knife, chopping board, electric whisk, basting brush, timer, colander, tin foil, fork, large metal spoon, carving knife

Set the oven to 200 degrees Celsius (400 degrees Fahrenheit).

Step 2: Ingredients ready

For the roast turkey

1 rolled turkey (dark meat only)*

1 tablespoon olive oil

1 teaspoon coarse salt

½ teaspoon cinnamon

Pinch of ground nutmeg

2 tablespoons honey

* A butcher should be able to make this up for you.

For the sweet potato mash

1 regular medium-sized potato, peeled and chopped

3 large sweet potatoes, peeled and chopped

1 tablespoon coarse salt

Step 3: Preparing the turkey

Place the turkey roll on a wire rack resting on a roasting tin.

Rub the roll with the olive oil. Sprinkle the salt, cinnamon and nutmeg over the roll and rub them in.

Drizzle the honey over the top.

Step 4: Roasting the turkey

Put the turkey near the top of the oven and set the timer for 20 minutes.

When the timer beeps, turn the oven down to 180 degrees Celsius (350 degrees Fahrenheit). Reset the timer for 30 minutes.

When the timer beeps again, open the oven and ask an adult helper to remove the turkey and roasting tin.

Dip the basting brush in the gravy that has collected in the roasting tin and brush the turkey well with the gravy. **Take care not to splash yourself with the hot gravy.**

Put the turkey (on the wire rack) and the roasting tin of gravy back in the oven (ask an adult helper to do this if needed) and reset the timer for 20 minutes.

When the timer beeps again, repeat the basting step and return the turkey and the gravy to the oven. Then reset the timer for a further 10 minutes.

When the timer beeps, remove everything from the oven, turn the oven off, and baste the turkey again. When the turkey is cooked a dark golden gravy should have developed under the turkey, and when pierced with a knife the juices in the turkey should run clear.

Reset the timer and leave the turkey to rest under some tin foil for 10 minutes.

Step 5: Preparing the mash

While the turkey is roasting, put the potato and sweet potatoes in a saucepan and cover them with water.

Turn on the hob to high. Put the saucepan on the hob, cover with a lid and bring to the boil.

Remove the lid and add the salt, then lower the heat to medium and set the timer for 20 minutes.

When the timer beeps, turn off the hob, drain the cooked potatoes into a colander (ask a grown-up helper if needed) in the sink and then return them to the saucepan.

Drizzle with a little olive oil and whisk with the electric whisk until smooth.

Step 6: Slicing the turkey

Baste the turkey again and transfer it to a chopping board by wedging a fork inside it and supporting it with a large metal spoon from underneath.

Gently slice the turkey into 1cm (½ inch) slices.

Step 7: Presentation

Spoon some mashed potatoes on the plates and add 2 slices of turkey per person. Spoon some of the delicious gravy over the meat and potatoes.

Your thoughts or comments

....

....

....

....

Crunchy Apple and Raspberry Crumble

A sweet crunchy crumble on top of soft, bubbling hot fruit is the perfect dessert when you feel like having a filling meal. Wow your family and friends with this all-time classic!

Step 1: Equipment ready

Knife, chopping board, peeler, measuring cups, measuring spoons, mixing bowl, baking tin, timer

Set the oven to 180 degrees Celsius (350 degrees Fahrenheit).

Step 2: Ingredients ready

4 apples

1 teaspoon lemon juice

1 cup raspberries

4 tablespoons golden sugar

4 tablespoons dark
brown sugar

1 cup wholemeal
(wholewheat) flour

1 teaspoon ground cinnamon

3 tablespoons
ground almonds

½ cup butter

Step 3: Peeling and slicing

Cut each apple into four quarters.

Lie each quarter on its side and slice straight down, cutting off the core.

Carefully peel or cut the skin off each quarter and then cut each quarter into another four slices.

Put the apple slices in the baking tin. Drizzle the lemon juice over the apples and toss them around a little – the lemon juice will stop the apples going brown while you prepare the crumble.

Add the raspberries to the apples and mix them in evenly.

Step 4: Measuring and crumbling

Put the sugar, flour, cinnamon and ground almonds in a mixing bowl.

Cut the butter into chunks and add to the mixing bowl.

Crumble the flour mixture with the butter by rubbing your finger tips against your thumbs.

Step 5: Preparing the crumble for baking

Sprinkle handfuls of crumble all over the fruit. Begin by spreading a thin layer so the apples and raspberries are covered, then double up the layer of crumble until the fruit is thickly covered.

Put your apple crumble in the top part of the oven and set the timer for 45 minutes.

When the timer beeps, check to see if your dish is ready – the crumble should look crunchy and the apples will be tender and bubbling.

When the crumble is ready, turn off the oven.

Step 6: Presentation

Serve hot with a dollop of Vanilla Ice Cream (see page 150).

Your thoughts or comments

....

....

....

....

Cinnamon Pancakes with Maple Syrup Butter

Everyone has their favourite way of enjoying sweet pancakes.

Whether you like them mixed with fresh fruit, or drizzled with maple syrup or chocolate sauce, here is a healthy, delicious pancake recipe that you will want to make over and over again.

Step 1: Equipment ready

Large mixing bowl, measuring cups, measuring spoons, knife, large hand whisk, frying pan, ice cream scoop, flat spatula

Step 2: Ingredients ready

200ml (7fl oz) pot of 3% fat plain bio yogurt

½ cup full fat milk

2 large eggs

2 tablespoons vegetable oil

1 cup wholemeal (wholewheat) flour

3 tablespoons golden brown sugar

2 teaspoons baking powder

¼ teaspoon coarse salt

½ teaspoon ground cinnamon

1 tablespoon olive oil for frying

Drizzle of maple syrup and a knob of butter for serving

Step 3: Start whisking

Put the yogurt, milk, eggs and vegetable oil in your mixing bowl and whisk until combined.

Step 4: Measuring and whisking

Measure the flour, sugar, baking powder, salt and ground cinnamon and add to the mixing bowl.

Continue whisking until combined. It's okay to have a few lumps!

Step 5: Frying and flipping

Heat the olive oil in a frying pan on a medium heat.

Add an ice cream scoop full of batter to the pan. Use the back of the scoop to gently shape the batter into an even circle. Wait for bubbles to appear in the batter and begin to pop.

Hold the frying pan with one hand, and with the other hand slide the spatula carefully underneath the whole pancake. Lift and flip the pancake over.

Leave to cook for 10 seconds, then using the spatula, remove the pancake from the pan.

Repeat with the rest of the pancake batter. (You can add a little more olive oil to the pan in between frying if you need to.)

Turn off the hob.

Step 6: Presentation

Stack your pancakes on top of each other in the centre of a plate.

Add a small knob of butter to the top pancake and drizzle with maple syrup. Alternatively, you might enjoy these pancakes with slices of banana or some fresh blueberries.

Your thoughts or comments

....

....

....

....

My First Chocolate Cake

Making a first chocolate cake is a celebration in itself — a great achievement and a perfect way to finish your cookery course.

Make it every time you celebrate someone's birthday or a happy time in your life.

Skills used: measuring cups, measuring spoons, electric whisk, boiling, oven, hot food, presentation

Preparation time: 25 minutes

Cooking time: 50–55 minutes

Step 1: Equipment ready

2 mixing bowls, measuring cups, measuring spoons, sieve, round 20cm (8 inch) cake tin, baking paper, small saucepan, hand whisk, electric whisk, wire rack, cake spatula, timer

Set the oven to 160 degrees Celsius (315 degrees Fahrenheit).

Step 2: Ingredients ready

For the cake

1 cup butter	1 teaspoon baking powder
1 cup caster sugar	1 cup cocoa
½ cup ground almonds	3 large eggs
½ cup self raising flour	

For the glaze

1 cup whipping cream	1 cup chocolate chips

Step 3: Making the cake batter

Put the butter and sugar in a mixing bowl. Using the electric whisk on a low setting beat the butter and sugar together until fluffy and lighter in colour.

In a separate mixing bowl sieve together the ground almonds, flour, baking powder and cocoa.

Add ⅓ of the flour mixture to the butter and sugar and whisk on a low setting.

Add 1 egg and continue whisking.

Add another ⅓ of the flour mixture and whisk again.

Add another egg, then flour, then the third egg and whisk again.

Remove the electric whisk and use a cake spatula to scrape down the sides of the bowl, making sure that all the ingredients are combined. Whisk one more time if necessary.

Step 4: Baking the cake

Pour the batter into the prepared cake tin and scrape down the sides of the mixing bowl with the spatula.

Put the cake into the lower part of the oven.

Set the timer for 50–55 minutes.

When the timer beeps, turn the oven off, carefully remove the cake from the oven and leave to cool completely.

Step 5: Making the glaze

Turn on the hob to a medium–low heat.

Put the whipping cream in a saucepan and heat until just boiling.

Remove from the heat and add the chocolate chips, whisking with a hand whisk until fully combined.

Sometimes the top of a cake isn't completely flat so simply turn the cake out from the tin and lay it upside down on a wire rack that is resting on baking paper.

Slowly pour the chocolate glaze over the cake and, using the cake spatula, gently spread the glaze over and down the sides of the cake until the whole cake is coated.

Step 6: Presentation

Slide the spatula underneath the cake and slowly lift and transfer it to a cake stand.

Decorate with your topping of choice, such as hundreds and thousands, chocolate buttons, Smarties or jelly sweets.

Celebrate with your first chocolate cake!

Your thoughts or comments

....

....

....

....

Menu Ideas

Now that you have had experience cooking such a wide variety of dishes you can start exploring and combining different dishes that complement each other, to make a full meal.
Here are some menu plans to get you started:

Minestrone Soup

followed by

Loaded Potatoes

Cheesy Popeye Pancakes

served with

chopped fresh vegetables dipped in hummus

followed by

Fruit Mountain

Pizza: The Italiano

served with

Wild West Wedges for an afternoon with friends

followed by

Sticky Chocolate Cornflakes

Ocean Fishcakes

served with

Quick Mushroom and Pea Risotto

followed by

Fruit Mountain

Farfallino Pasta

followed by

Gooey Chocolate Brownie

with a scoop of Vanilla Ice Cream

Aunty Deb's Choc Chunk Cookies

served with

a cup of hot chocolate

Fish Fingers

served with

Crispy Mac 'n' Cheese

Lentil Soup

followed by

Creamy Chicken Sandwich

Invite friends to tea and serve Baker's Bread sandwiches

followed by

Classic Victoria Sponge cake

Simply Perfect Roast Chicken with Basmati Rice
served with
Sweet and Sour Cabbage

Classic Chicken Noodle Soup
followed by
Simply Perfect Roast Chicken with Basmati Rice

Bolognese
followed by
Fruit Mountain

Enjoy Cinnamon Pancakes for Sunday
breakfast with all the family
topped with
fresh fruit and sauces of your choice

**Make My First Chocolate Cake to celebrate
the birthday of someone you love**

Honey–roasted Turkey with Sweet Potato Mash
followed by
Crunchy Apple and Raspberry Crumble
with a scoop of Vanilla Ice Cream

Index

America, hot dogs 27
apples 18
    making juice 22
athletes, choosing foods
    34–9
Aunty Deb's choc chunk
    cookies 114–17
Australia, Pavlova dessert
    26

baked potatoes 99–101
baker's bread 89–92
baking, equipment 63–4
baking paper 63
baking trays 60
basmati rice 158–60
basting brush 64
batter, mixing 71–2
beans 29, 32
beef
    bolognese 175–8
    ultimate burger 172–4
best before dates 49
biscuits, Aunty Deb's
    choc chunk cookies
    114–17
boiling 78
bolognese 175–8
book, background to
    11–12
bread 28, 30, 89–92
    cheesy garlic bread
    134–7
brownies 153–5
burger 172–4

cabbage, sweet and sour
    cabbage 165–8
cake cases 64

cake tins 60
cakes
    classic victoria sponge
        146–9
    gooey chocolate
        brownies 153–5
    my first chocolate cake
        189–92
    sticky chocolate
        cornflakes 112–14
calcium 32
carbohydrates 28, 30
cheesy garlic bread
    134–7
cheesy popeye pancakes
    96–8
chefs 44
chicken
    classic chicken noodle
        soup 161–4
    creamy chicken
        sandwich 169–71
    crunchy chicken with
        sweet and sour
        cabbage 165–8
    simply perfect roast
        chicken with
        basmati rice
        158–60
    storing 50–1
chicken noodle soup
    161–4
chives 124
choc chunk cookies
    114–17
chocolate brownies
    153–5
chocolate cake 189–92

choosing foods 34–41
    and cooking them 46
chopping boards 54, 62
cinnamon pancakes with
    maple syrup butter
    186–8
classic chicken noodle
    soup 161–4
classic victoria sponge
    146–9
cleanliness 54, 55
cloths, cleanliness 55
colanders 59
cooked chicken and meat
    reheating 51
    storing 51
cookies, Aunty Deb's
    choc chunk cookies
    114–17
cooking
    and being independent
        47
    benefits of learning 46
    and choosing foods 41
    and concentration 11
    and food choices 46
    and helping other
        people 47
    learning 44, 45
    making friends 46
    meaning of 41–3
    as shared activity 12
cooking process,
    elements of 12–13
cooks, who they are and
    what they do 44
corn 18
countries, different foods
    24–7

cows 16
cream tea 26
creamy chicken sandwich 169–71
creamy scrambled eggs with smoked salmon 124–6
crispy mac 'n' cheese 130–3
cross-contamination 53
crunchy apple and raspberry crumble 183–5
crunchy chicken with sweet and sour cabbage 165–8
cupboard ingredients, storing 52
curry 26

dairy foods 28, 32
David, choosing foods 36, 38
desserts
    crunchy apple and raspberry crumble 183–5
    fruit mountain 109–11
    vanilla ice cream 150–2
diet, and fitness 35–9
dos and don'ts, kitchen safety 56–8
double bedded eggs 93–5
dry ingredients, storing 52

Eat Well plate 28–9
egg cracking 73
eggs 29, 32
    creamy scrambled eggs with smoked salmon 124–6
    double bedded eggs 93–5
electric whisking 74
electric whisks 63
equipment 59–65

farfallino pasta 105–8
farms 16
fatty foods 28–9, 33
fish 17, 29, 32, 119
    creamy scrambled eggs with smoked salmon 124–6
    fish fingers with wild west wedges 142–5
    fishcakes 138–41
    preparing 21
fish fingers with wild west wedges 142–5
fitness, and diet 35–9
food, sources 15–19
food groups, healthy diet 28–33
food preparation
    equipment 62
    safety 53
foods, getting ready to eat or drink 20–3
fridges
    packing 55
    storing food 50–2
frozen foods, storing 50
fruit mountain 109–11
fruits 29, 31
    fruit mountain 109–11
    storing 52
frying 79
    equipment 60
frying pans 61

gardening 19
gooey chocolate brownies 153–5
grains 18
    making into bread 23
graters 62
grating 68
growing food in your garden 19

hamburger 172–4
hand mixing 69
hand whisking 74

hand whisks 63
handwashing 55, 56
healthy diet 28–33
    choosing foods 34–41
    eating enough 35–9
heat 14, 76–7
helping other people 47
Henry, starting to cook 11–12
honey roasted turkey with sweet potato mash 179–82
hot dogs 27
hot food, safety 77

ice cream, vanilla ice cream 150–2
ice cream scoops 64
Icon and Skill Glossary 13
icons
    boiling 78
    egg cracking 73
    electric whisking 74
    frying 79
    grating 68
    hand mixing 69
    hand whisking 74
    heat 76–7
    hot food 77
    kneading 70
    knife 66–7
    measuring cups 75
    measuring spoons 76
    metal spoon mixing 72
    oven 79
    peeling 67
    presentation 80
    timing 80
independence 47
India, curry 26
ingredients, ways of using 23–7

Japan, sushi 27
Julia, choosing foods 37, 39

keeping safe
  food preparation 53
  kitchen dangers 54–5
  storing food 48–52
kettles 59
kitchen dangers 54–5
  dos and don'ts 56–8
kneading 70
knife icon 66–7
knives 62
  allowing use of 12
  skills 66–7

lentil soup with cheesy
    garlic bread 134–7
level one recipes 85–117
  Aunty Deb's choc chunk
    cookies 114–17
  baker's bread 89–92
  cheesy popeye
    pancakes 96–8
  double bedded eggs
    93–5
  farfallino pasta 105–8
  fruit mountain 109–11
  loaded potatoes
    99–101
  minestrone madness
    102–4
  peckish pita pieces
    86–8
  sticky chocolate
    cornflakes 112–14
level two recipes 119–55
  classic victoria sponge
    146–9
  creamy scrambled
    eggs with smoked
    salmon 124–6
  crispy mac 'n' cheese
    130–3
  fish fingers with wild
    west wedges 142–5
  gooey chocolate
    brownies 153–5
  lentil soup with cheesy
    garlic bread 134–7
  ocean fishcakes 138–41

pizza italiano 120–3
quick mushroom and
    pea risotto 127–9
vanilla ice cream 150–2
level three recipes
    157–92
  bolognese 175–8
  cinnamon pancakes
    with maple syrup
    butter 186–8
  classic chicken noodle
    soup 161–4
  creamy chicken
    sandwich 169–71
  crunchy apple and
    raspberry crumble
    183–5
  honey roasted turkey
    with sweet potato
    mash 179–82
  my first chocolate cake
    189–92
  simply perfect roast
    chicken with
    basmati rice
    158–60
  ultimate burger 172–4
loaded potatoes 99–101
loaf tins 60

mac 'n' cheese 130–3
maple syrup butter
    186–8
measuring cups 63, 75
measuring ingredients 14
measuring spoons 63, 76
meat 29, 32
  bolognese 175–8
  storing 50–1
  ultimate burger 172–4
menu ideas 193–5
metal spoon mixing 72
metal spoons 63
Middle East, traditional
    foods 27
milk 20, 28, 32
minerals in foods 32

minestrone madness
    102–4
mixing
  hand mixing 69
  metal spoon mixing 72
  wooden spoon mixing
    71
mixing bowls 63
my first chocolate cake
    189–92

ocean fishcakes 138–41
oven 60, 79
oven cooking, equipment
    60
oven gloves 65, 77, 79
  cleanliness 55
oven temperatures 14

pancakes, cheesy popeye
    pancakes 96–8
pasta 28, 30
  bolognese 175–8
  crispy mac 'n' cheese
    130–3
  farfallino pasta 105–8
pasta sauces
  bolognese 175–8
  tomato 105–8
Pavlova dessert 26
peckish pita pieces 86–8
peeler icon 67
peelers 62
peeling 67
pita pieces 86–8
pizza italiano 120–3
potatoes 18, 28, 30
  loaded potatoes
    99–101
  wild west wedges
    142–5
presentation 80
proteins 29, 32

quick mushroom and pea
    risotto 127–9

raw chicken and meat
  safety 54
  storing 50–1
recipes
  categories 13
  layout and explanation 81–3
  levels 14
  presentation 13
reheating, cooked chicken and meat 51
rice 28, 30
  quick mushroom and pea risotto 127–9
  simply perfect roast chicken with basmati rice 158–60
risotto, quick mushroom and pea risotto 127–9
roast chicken with basmati rice 158–60
rolling boil 78
rubbish bins 55
rye 18

safety 157
  boiling 78
  dos and don'ts 56–8
  food preparation 53
  frying 79
  hot food 77
  kitchen dangers 54–5
  oven 79
  storing food 48–52
sandwiches
  creamy chicken sandwich 169–71
  ultimate burger 172–4
saucepans 59
shelf life 48–52
sieves 64
simmering 78
simply perfect roast chicken with basmati rice 158–60

skills
  boiling 78
  egg cracking 73
  electric whisking 73–4
  frying 79
  grating 68
  hand mixing 69
  hand whisking 74
  heat 76–7
  kneading 70
  knives 66–7
  measuring 75–6
  metal spoon mixing 72
  oven 79
  peeling 67
  presentation 80
  timing 80
  wooden spoon mixing 71
soup ladles 59
soups
  classic chicken noodle soup 161–4
  lentil soup with cheesy garlic bread 134–7
  minestrone madness 102–4
spatulas 61
spoiled food 50
spoons 63
sticky chocolate cornflakes 112–14
storing food 48–52
  cupboard ingredients 52
  dry ingredients 52
  in the fridge 50–2
  frozen foods 50
sugary foods 28–9, 33
sushi 27
sweet and sour cabbage 165–8
sweet potato mash 179–82

temperatures 14
timers 65
timing 80
tin foil 65
towels 65
  cleanliness 55
trying new foods 85
tuna fishcakes 138–41
turkey, honey roasted turkey with sweet potato mash 179–82

ultimate burger 172–4
United Kingdom, cream tea 26
use by dates 49

vanilla ice cream 150–2
vegetables 31
  storing 52
victoria sponge 146–9

washing up 54
wheat 18
where food comes from 15–19
whisking
  electric whisking 74
  hand whisking 74
wholegrains 30
wild west wedges 142–5
wire racks 60
wooden spoon mixing 71
wooden spoons 63